ING
)AY
and
)AY

PREACHING
YESTERDAY
AND TODAY

Henry E. Walter Ltd.
and
Carey Publications Ltd.

BV
7222
.E83
1971

PPR

ISBN 0 85479 630 4

First printed 1972

Printed by
University Tutorial Press Ltd.
Foxton, near Cambridge, England
for
Henry E. Walter Ltd., 26 Grafton Road, Worthing
Carey Publications Ltd.
5 Fairford Close, Haywards Heath,
Sussex RH16 3EF.

CONTENTS

About the Authors

Jim van Zyl—

Is the minister of the Hill Crest Baptist Church, Natal. He studied at the Baptist College in Johannesburg and the University of Port Elizabeth. He has been Associate minister of Trinity Baptist Church in Port Elizabeth and also pastored an Evangelical Presbyterian Church in Northern Ireland. An able writer and organiser, he has pioneered in the field of promoting Biblical literature among African peoples. He was chiefly instrumental in organising the first Evangelical and Reformed Studies Conference in South Africa at Port Elizabeth where the idea was born that the papers, if brought together and edited for publication, would be of help to many.

David Kingdon—

Is principal of the Irish Baptist College, Belfast, Northern Ireland. He studied at Cambridge University and Spurgeon's College. Noted for his formulative and penetrating thinking, he is gifted in preaching, lecturing, debating and writing.

Jannie du Preez—

Has been the Principal of the Dutch Reformed Church Theological School (N.G.Kerk), Umtata since 1960. He graduated from Stellenbosch University and was ordained in 1952. He is active in missionary work and trains Xhosa-speaking ministers for the work in the Transkel.
Dr. du Preez has travelled in Europe and is keenly aware of the need of revival among evangelical churches today.

Erroll Hulse—

Qualified as an architect at Pretoria University and subsequently studied at the London Bible College. Since 1962 he has been the minister of the Cuckfield Baptist Church. He is the editor of the quarterly magazine *Reformation Today*, and is known for his enthusiasm to promote expository literature in English and other languages.

Introduction

SOME CHRISTIANS ARE CONCERNED ABOUT THE LACK OF SPIRITUAL UNCTION, doctrinal structure and efficacy that there is in preaching today. They are concerned too about the paucity in number of those who experience a saving change in their lives compared with former times. It is commonly believed that the fault lies mainly in the realm of presentation and that methods of presenting the Gospel need modernising. The conviction of the writers of this book is that it is not so much the presentation of the Gospel, as the content of the message that requires reformation.

The first chapter on George Whitefield illustrates the relationship of Biblical doctrine to preaching, as well as its importance in regard to revival. Whitefield did not use evangelistic methods commonly employed today, yet he was favoured with extraordinary spiritual endowment throughout his ministry. Standing in the rain and cold, listening to Whitefield, was in all probability immensely more inspiring than sitting in an armchair watching Gospel entertainment on television! This is not to advocate the merit of cold or rain or to reject the value of Gospel programmes on television, but rather a reminder of the reality and power of the Holy Spirit in using truth which is foolishness to men, but power to God.

Whitefield is an excellent example too, of what it is to hold the doctrines of grace in practice. It is necessary to say *in practice* because not a few hold them in theory only. Great courage and faith is needed to preach these truths and, at the same time, resist artificial procedures, pressures and methods designed to obtain visible results which may flatter the evangelist's record, but in the process of time prove to fall short of regeneration.

The second chapter concerning free will, introduces a subject which is not an academic debating point, but an issue of fundamental importance to the Gospel. God's grace and free will are not different aspects of the same truth. They represent incompatible theologies, the one alien to the other. There is a world of difference between free will and human responsibility.

How can we evangelise if the sinner's will is not free but in bondage to sin? Whitefield seemed not to have this problem but Jim van Zyl enters into detail and shows with cogency that it is untrue and inaccurate to allege that free grace belief hinders evangelism.

With the contemporary situation very much in mind David Kingdon expounds the subject of evangelism and shows how shortcomings in evangelistic outreach result directly from an inadequate grasp of the nature of man and sin. He suggests positive measures to restore a more Biblical pattern for evangelism.

In the next chapter he shows that the mind of modern man is essentially materialistic in outlook: autonomous, antisupernaturalistic, this-worldly and antiauthoritarian. As Christianity meets the secular world head-on, important issues come to the fore, such as man's pretended autonomy. Positive suggestions are placed before the reader as to practical measures that can be taken to strengthen the presentation of the Gospel as it is proclaimed in a secular society.

Very often preaching is evangelistic, but lacking in doctrine and depth. This militates against its effectiveness. Jannie du Preez points to the necessity of Biblical, expository and doctrinal preaching. He shows just how much is involved if God is to be honoured in exposition which is worthy of the Scriptures from which it purports to come. Failure at the point of exposition will result in a parallel impoverishment in every other field of the Church's life, thought and witness.

These papers are presented in an order which first looks at the past and then with detail at our present needy world. They were read at the first Evangelical and Reformed Conference in South Africa which took place at Port Elizabeth in April, 1971. Not all the papers are reproduced here. They were all edifying, but the demands of pastoral responsibility make it impossible for all to be edited for printing. Particularly missed is the stimulating and convicting paper by the Rev. A. S. Gilfillan on Expository Preaching, in which he stressed the necessity of "relevance" in preaching.

It is the earnest prayer of the authors that these chapters should contribute toward renewed efforts to attain high standards in preaching and a hunger for revival. May the Holy Spirit use them to that end.

REVIVAL, PREACHING, and the DOCTRINES OF GRACE illustrated from the life of GEORGE WHITEFIELD

Erroll Hulse

GEORGE WHITEFIELD IS REGARDED BY DR. MARTYN LLOYD-JONES AS "the greatest preacher England has ever produced".[1] J. C. Ryle said of him that he was "entirely chief and first among the English Reformers of the 18th century".[2] In the new biography of George Whitefield, a work of considerable research, Arnold Dallimore describes Whitefield as "the foremost figure of the immense religious movement that held the attention of multitudes on both sides of the Atlantic",[3] while Spurgeon testified that "he felt quickening every time he studied Whitefield"[4] and made him his model.[5]

The life of Whitefield is important for us today because through him we are reminded of the reality of true revival. In a time when many false ideas are circulated, and when many reports are made purporting the phenomena of revival, it is vital for us to maintain Biblical and historical concepts of what revival is. Furthermore, our day is one in which we find a great deal of entertainment existing in the evangelical churches. There is what is known as "entertainment evangelism". Much manipulation is used to produce a visible response in the work of evangelism. The ministry of George Whitefield stands in strong contrast to the approach and methods used today.

Moreover in Whitefield's ministry we see the primacy of preaching and the relevance of Whitefield for our day is seen in the fact that he was a fearless preacher of what we call "the doctrines of grace". Our era is one in which the message of the Gospel is watered down, made effeminate, and emasculated of those characteristics which make it strong and robust. In contrast to this, Whitefield's Gospel rippled with that power which melts the inward man and turns the whole soul in repentance to God. Like Paul he proclaimed the whole counsel of Jehovah.

I propose to sketch Whitefield's life and then proceed to deal with the three main factors which are of major importance for us today. The plan then is to provide an outline of Whitefield's life and character and to illustrate from his life the following factors: 1. The fact of revival. 2. The primacy of preaching. 3. The importance of the doctrines of grace.

A brief outline of Whitefield's life and character

Whitefield was born in 1714 at Gloucester, where his parents were the proprietors of the Bell Inn. His father died when George was young and his mother thereafter had much difficulty in keeping the inn well organised. George was taken from Grammar School when he was fifteen in order to assist with work at the inn. This period lasted about a year and a half. The young man was intelligent and his friends felt it worth while to seek a place for him at Pembroke College, Oxford. Here it was that George first met John and Charles Wesley. He joined the "Holy Club" and at this early period of his life he was gripped by strong ascetic and mystical ideas of Christianity. Through reading Puritan literature he soon became immersed in the Bible itself. The main Puritan authors of help to him were Scougal, Baxter, Joseph Alleine and Matthew Henry. He spent many hours a day praying over the Scriptures and was, in these formulative years, to rely much on Matthew Henry for guidance as to the meaning of the text. In due course he turned completely from legalism, asceticism and perfectionism. Ryle says "of all the little band of Oxford Methodists, none seemed to have got hold so soon of clear views of Christ's Gospel as he did, and none kept it so unwaveringly to the end".[6]

Whitefield was ordained in Gloucester at the age of twenty-two where he preached his first sermon. A pointer to his unusual character and ability was seen in that a complaint was made that fifteen people had been driven mad by the sermon. The Bishop had the good sense to reply "that he wished that the madness might not be forgotten before the next Sunday!"[7]

Following this the young preacher went back to Oxford for a short period and from there began to preach in several churches in London where his presentation of the Gospel caused an immense sensation. To quote Ryle again: "A really eloquent, extempore preacher, preaching the pure Gospel with the most uncommon gifts of voice and manner, was at that time an entire novelty in London".[8]

The excitement in London was followed by a two months period of comparative quietness in the village parish of Dunmer.

His contact and friendship with John Wesley had quickened ideas about going to Georgia as a missionary. His ambition was to establish an orphanage in the New World and at this time in his early career the way was opened for him to make his first crossing of the Atlantic. But to give a more precise idea of the position at this time when Whitefield was twenty-two years of age I quote Luke Tyerman:

"Whitefield wished and expected to embark for Georgia without delay; but by a series of unforeseen occurrences, he was detained in England during the whole of the year 1737. In some respects this was the most important period of his life. He had transferred the care of the prisoners at Oxford to Dean Kinchin. James Hervey had succeeded him in the curacy at Dunmer. He had no parochial charge, and probably he wished for none. At the early age of twenty-two, he was an episcopally ordained evangelist, ready and eager to preach whenever and wherever an opportunity of doing so was presented. The year was spent in a continued succession of public services, which literally startled the nation. He was a new phenomenon in the Church of England. All eyes were fixed upon him. His popularity in Bristol, London, and other places was enormous. His preaching became the subject of public remark; his name, hitherto almost entirely unknown, became a household word. Thousands and tens of thousands were making enquiries concerning him. His position was perilous. Popular favour might have ruined him; but the grace of God preserved him. This year's evangelistic labours in England gave a bias to the whole of his future life. Never afterwards did he desire church preferment. As an ordained clergyman, the whole of his subsequent career was irregular. He was a Gospel rover. No power on earth could confine him to a single parish or a single church." [9]

The latter description of Whitefield, particularly the last few sentences concerning his work as a travelling preacher, aptly describes the rest of his life. Most of his ministry was attended by the mighty reviving power of the Holy Spirit and reference will be made in the next section to this particular aspect. [10] But now to give further idea of the great preacher of the 18th century we need to examine some aspects of his character which might help provide a fuller picture of the man.

His Appearance
Whitefield was about average height, slender in his youth but corpulent after the age of forty which was due to ill-health and not over-eating. He was frugal in his eating habits. His complexion was fair. Those who mocked his Gospel used to call him "Mr. Squintum", on account of the pronounced squint of his dark, small, lively, blue eyes. Gillies, a contemporary historian, has the following description: "Manly countenance, his voice exceedingly strong; yet both were softened with an uncommon degree of sweetness. He was always very clean and neat and often said presently that a minister of the Gospel ought to be without spot". [11] Whitefield had a warm yet polite manner which made his company well liked and acceptable. In his conversation he was cheerful, communicative and entertaining. He was accessible to the most humble people and ever ready to help those in need, either spiritually or practically. [12]

His Catholicity of Spirit
Much hated by the unconverted clergy Whitefield never compromised the Gospel. On some occasions he was very outspoken against ministers unqualified in this respect. Yet he maintained a generous and affectionate attitude to all believers. In America he worked mainly with dissenters and often had a Baptist minister to assist him.

An illustration of his catholic spirit is found in his dealings with "The Associate Presbytery of Scotland". This was a secession group of ministers who felt very strongly about the apostasy within the Church of Scotland. It contained well-known preachers such as Ralph and Ebenezer Erskine. These ministers invited Whitefield to preach for them but desired that he should confine his efforts to their congregations. Whitefield's description of what occurred best describes the situation and illustrates his own broad-minded outlook:

"I met most of them according to appointment, on Wednesday last. A set of grave, venerable men! They soon proposed to form them-

4

selves into a presbytery, and were proceeding to choose a moderator. I asked them for what purpose? They answered, to discourse, and set me right about the matter of church government, and the Solemn League and Covenant. I replied, they might save themselves the trouble, for I had no scruples about it; and that settling church government, and preaching about the Solemn League and Covenant, was not my plan. I then told them something of my experience, and how I was led out into my present way of acting. One, in particular, said he was deeply affected; and dear Mr. Erskine desired they would have patience with me; for that, having been born and bred in England, and having never studied the point, I could not be supposed to be so perfectly acquainted with the nature of the covenants. One, much warmer than the rest, immediately replied, 'that no indulgence was to be shewn me; that England had revolted most with respect to church government; and that I, born and educated there, could not but be acquainted with the matter now in debate'. I told him, I had never yet made the Solemn League and Covenant the object of my study, being busy about matters, as I judged, of greater importance. Several replied that every pin of the tabernacle was precious. I said, that, in every building there were outside and inside workmen; that the latter, at present, was my province; that if they thought themselves called to the former, they might proceed in their own way, and I should proceed in mine. I then asked them seriously, what they would have me to do? The answer was, that I was not desired to subscribe immediately to the Solemn League and Covenant, but to preach only for them till I had further light. I asked, why only for them? Mr. Ralph Erskine said, 'they were the Lord's people'. I then asked, whether there were no other Lord's people but themselves; and, supposing all others were devil's people, they certainly had more need to be preached to; and, therefore, I was more and more determined to go out into the highways and hedges; and that, if the Pope himself would lend me his pulpit, I would gladly proclaim the righteousness of Jesus Christ therein." [13]

The above incident resulted in a breach which grieved Whitefield at heart. He proceeded to serve the needs of the Church of Scotland and God was pleased to pour out the Holy Spirit in a mighty awakening subsequent to this time.

This anecdote is not quoted to be used as a vindication of the ecumenical movement or to encourage compromise. In our day the situation is very different from that of the 18th century when the large non-conformist denominations were basically evangelical and orthodox in faith.

A Sense of Social Righteousness
There may be substance to the claim that Whitefield was hindered in his main work of preaching by having to bear the responsibility of the orphanage. This often seemed an intolerable burden to him right up

to within two years of his death, when he was finally freed from debt. He launched into the orphanage work when he was only 24, a step which followed two years of planning. The enterprise was a vision of the Holy Club and Whitefield vainly thought that most associates of the Club were behind him. Alas, as is often the case, dreaming great things is not the same as doing them. Others dreamed, he was left to the doing.

But was the orphanage a mistake? Did it hinder Whitefield in his preaching? The answer to this must surely be seen in the observation that life consists of a blend of activities. If these are in harmony and proportion then each department will assist the other. Faith without works is dead. Every pastor knows the difficulty of dividing time so as to do justice to study, to preaching, to visitation, to family responsibilities, and to the proper development and use of any special gift for service that there may be. The orphanage did hinder Whitefield from time to time. But then we should remember that works of righteousness greatly enriched his testimony. For instance on his fifth visit to America he took with him twenty-two destitute children who were to discover new life in America. Surely some of these will rise up to thank God for their benefactor in the day of judgment.

Whitefield's burden for the Negroes expressed itself in an endeavour to start a school for them as well as a settlement for persecuted people which he attempted in 1740. The death of his young friend and companion, William Seward, a wealthy young financier, extinguished this hope. Seward had guaranteed £2,200 for the venture. Whitefield did not hesitate to be very direct in his application while preaching in America and rebuked landowners for the misuse of their slaves by exposition of the text James 5:4, "Behold, the hire of the labourers who have reaped down your fields, which is of you kept back by fraud, crieth: and the cries of them which have reaped are entered into the ears of the Lord of sabaoth".

From these facets of the preacher's character we turn now to three main lessons which can be illustrated from his life.

1. The fact of revival

Two specific dangers face us today. The first is to be infatuated with and deceived by exaggerated reports of religious excitement purported to be revival. From various parts of the world we hear of miracles and of many people making decisions for Christ. Closer investigation of some of these movements shows that much is to be desired and that the activity is often predominantly unbiblical and even spurious. The

Scriptures teach us that we must discern between the false and the true.[14] There are "neo" Christs, "neo" Pentecosts and "neo" revivals. There is a need, therefore, to have a clear idea of what revival really is. The second danger is to become cynical because so much time has elapsed since the last widespread awakening which took place in 1859. In the face of shallowness, error and discouragement, it is possible for true believers to begin to doubt the reality of revival altogether and to think exclusively in terms of a long uphill labour. It is right that we should face the reality of having to persevere through times of discouragement but wrong to become sceptical about revival. To cease to regard it as a possibility, and therefore to cease to pray for it at all, would be a serious mistake. We are to seek and expect great things from God.

One cannot read closely into the life of George Whitefield and into the details of the Great Awakening without being impressed by the reality of an outpouring of the Holy Spirit. Let us now look at the social conditions that prevailed at that time and then observe the way in which God intervened.

In some quarters of London every sixth house was a gin den, while immorality in all parts of society was appalling.[15] It could be said of Moorfields and Kennington Common that wild beasts are better mannered, cleaner and more desirable company than the vile devils of these parks, whose chief delight seemed to be the reproach of their Creator. To maintain law and order severe penalties were imposed upon offenders. It was not unusual for citizens to be hanged in public for petty offences and a common sight to see revelries going on against a backdrop of dangling corpses.

To illustrate the crude nature of conditions, an incident can be cited from the life of Joseph Periam one of Whitefield's converts. After conversion he was unjustly sentenced to the madhouse by relatives who hated the Gospel. Three symptoms were stated as the reason for this drastic action: 1. He had fasted for a fortnight. 2. He had prayed so loud as to be heard all over a house four storeys high! 3. He had sold his clothes to give his money to the poor.[16]

In this asylum the prisoners were chained naked to their walls and an entrance fee was paid by the public as a form of entertainment. £400 a year was collected by this means, a practice not abolished until 1770. This illustrates something of the moral ugliness of the period.

Moorfields consisted of an eighteen-acre common with rows of stalls where the people could indulge in bear baiting, cudgel fighting, wrestling, dog fights or watching "Merry-Andrew" shows at their leisure. For lack of positive activity thousands of people whiled away their time at Moorfields. Before the advent of Whitefield's preaching at Moorfields some believers of the Fetter Lane Society had experimented with open-air preaching. For their trouble they had had their table broken into fragments and had had to run for their lives.

In this situation, Whitefield, with the help of his friends gained a foothold and once the sermon was under way he was able to grip the attention of the people with such effect that large crowds increased daily until such numbers were reached that it would be difficult to refute the claim that these were the largest crowds ever to attend an unamplified human voice.[17]

What pertained at Moorfields applied also to Kennington Common, a twenty-acre park, which served as a drain for the dregs of humanity—a meeting place for the unwashed, ignorant, unkempt, diseased and wicked. When did the revival first break out? Some point to the first time open-air work was attempted. It was Howell Harris who encouraged Whitefield to engage in open-air preaching, and Kingswood, near Bristol, was the scene of the great preacher's first efforts. In this area large numbers of miners lived like rats in unspeakably squalid conditions. During February, 1739, in a winter which was known for its freezing conditions, Whitefield spent six weeks inviting people out of their dens and holes. The first congregation consisted of about 200. This steadily increased to 20,000. "The first discovery of their being affected was to see white gutters made by their tears which plentifully ran down their black cheeks as they came out of their coal pits. Hundreds were soon brought under deep conviction and as the event proved, happily ended in a sound and thorough conversion." [18]

The revival as a whole lasted in intensity for several years, perhaps a decade, from 1735, which is noteworthy because of the revival in New England, and at Northampton in particular. Of course it did not belong to any one man or group of men but was widespread as the following quotation will indicate:

"Mr. Whitefield, that man of God, came into this town last September, and preached with surprising success. Consolation and thunder were intermixed in all his discourses, so that numbers were made to cry out, 'What shall we do to be saved?' While the iron might be said to be hot, that Boanerges, Mr. Gilbert Tennent, came, and laboured with still greater success among us. Many hundreds of souls came under great distress. Lectures are set up and continued almost every day in the week. God's blessed Spirit is poured out on some of all ages and complexions. God has perfected praise from the mouths of many hundreds of children. Many poor Ethiopians are made to stretch out their hands to God. In my little congregation, 178 souls have applied to me, either to relate what God had done for them, or to ask direction how to manage under soul trouble. One thing I would notice, the work of

Christ has been greater since these men of God have gone hence; but they brought the sacred fire along with them, and now it is kindled into a divine flame. God has made many townships and ministers light tapers at our torches; namely, Roxburg, Brookline, Cambridge, Charleston, Ipswich, Newburg, Rhode Island, with many more towns through almost all the provinces of English America. I do not know that I have ever read anything like this blessed time since the apostles' days." [19]

The most intense time of evangelical conviction of sin and repentance was perhaps the revival which took place upon Whitefield's second visit to Scotland in 1742. The churches were for the most part in a deplorable condition. It is noteworthy that scarcely one of Whitefield's converts had fallen back since his first visit the previous year. Several towns outside Glasgow experienced quickenings of the Spirit, particularly Kilsyth and Cambuslang, where McCulloch, the minister, had preached a series of sermons on the new birth, and arranged a time when three days were set apart for prayer. It was upon the fourth day that 50 people were awakened and during the ensuing three months 300 were converted. Such was the hunger for truth that a sermon was required every day. The following description gives some idea of the revival that transpired upon Whitefield's visit to Cambuslang following the initial awakening under McCulloch:

"Yesterday morning, I preached at Glasgow, to a large congregation. At mid-day, I came to Cambuslang, and preached, at two, to a vast body of people; again at six, and again at nine at night. Such commotions, surely, were never heard of, especially at eleven o'clock at night. For an hour and a half, there were such weeping, and so many falling into such deep distress, expressed in various ways, as cannot be described. The people seemed to be slain in scores. Their agonies and cries were exceedingly affecting. Mr. McCulloch preached, after I had done, till past one in the morning; and then could not persuade the people to depart. In the fields, all night, might be heard the voice of prayer and praise." [20]

A description of the work at Kilsyth is similar and many other quotations could be given which indicate the overwhelming convictions of soul that came upon the people:

"On Tuesday, twice at Kilsyth, to 10,000; but such a commotion, I believe, you never saw. Oh, what agonies and cries were there! Last night, God brought me hither. A friend met me without the town, and welcomed me in the name of 20,000. The streets were all alarmed. By three o'clock this morning, people were coming to hear the Word of God. At seven, I preached to many, many thousands; and again this evening. Our Lord wounded them by scores. It is impossible to tell you what I

9

see. The work flies from parish to parish. Oh, what distressed souls have I beheld this day!"[21]

The difference between these scenes and those in which emotions are organised by a programme should be obvious.

2. The primacy of preaching

John Newton, in a funeral sermon, preached in his church at Olney, said: "I have had some opportunities of looking over the history of the Church in past ages, and I am not backward to say, that I have not read or heard of any person, since the days of the apostles, of whom it may more emphatically be said, 'He was a burning and shining light', than of the late Mr. Whitefield. The Lord gave him a manner of preaching which was peculiarly his own. He copied from none, and I never met anyone who could imitate him with success. Those who attempted generally made themselves disagreeable. Other ministers, perhaps, could preach the Gospel as clearly, and in general say the same things; but, I believe, no man living could say them in his way."

"I bless God", added the Olney curate, "that I have lived in the time of Mr. Whitefield. Many were the winter mornings in which I got up at four, to attend his Tabernacle discourses at five; and I have seen Moorfields as full of lanthorns at these times as, I suppose, the Haymarket is full of flambeaux on an opera night. If anyone were to ask me who was the second preacher I ever heard, I should be at some loss to answer; but, in regard to the first, Mr. Whitefield exceeded so far every other man of my time, that I should be at none. He was the original of popular preaching, and all our popular ministers are only his copies."[22]

A minister in Scotland who was well aware of the extraordinary way in which Whitefield was used said of him, "I often think that the Lord sent him here to teach me how to preach". One of the disadvantages that ministers have today is the lack of men of Whitefield's character to whom they can listen and from whom they can learn.

To Whitefield preaching was like the prophesying which is described in Ezekiel chapter 37. He preached with the authority of heaven while God used his words to raise the dead to life.

The character of his preaching was extraordinary. With fervent, melting love he transposed from his heart to his hearers the most earnest persuasiveness, intense love and longing desire for their salvation. His bearing, gesture and speech was the outward vehicle of inward passion. Mrs. Jonathan Edwards, writing to her brother, said of him, "He is a

10

born orator, you have already heard of his deep-toned yet clear and melodious voice. It is perfect music. It is wonderful to see what a spell he casts over an audience by proclaiming the simplest truths of the Bible. I have seen upwards of 1,000 people hang on his words with breathless silence, broken only by an occasional half suppressed sob".[23] Benjamin Franklin, the famous physicist, publisher and statesman of those times took the trouble to actually measure the distance to which Whitefield could cast his voice and calculated the numbers who could hear him. These experiments vindicated the facts recorded during those times, although it is admitted that there has always been a tendency to exaggerate the numbers present at meetings, which must be allowed for. Franklin described Whitefield as being able to preach in such a way that "every accent, every emphasis, every modulation of the voice was so perfectly well tuned and well placed, that without being interested in the subject, one could not help being pleased with the discourse".

In our days there has been much talk about being baptised with the Holy Spirit, but very little explanation of what that means. Whitefield was constantly filled with the Spirit by which all his faculties of intellect, affections and will, were enlarged, and empowered. There is nothing by way of tongue-speaking or the artificial stimulation of gifts by laying on of hands, deep breathings, sighings, or repetitions of the word "Jesus", that can be laid hold of by advocates of the present day neo-Pentecostal Movement in the life of Whitefield. It is true that his natural gifts were unusual but how are we to explain the use of these apart from the fact that here we have a man who was filled with faith and the Holy Ghost. The eye-witness Gillies not only describes his preaching but points to the key factor thus:

"He had a strong and musical voice, and a wonderful command of it. His pronunciation was not only proper, but manly and graceful. He was never at a loss for the most natural and strong expressions. The grand sources of his eloquence were an exceeding lively imagination, and an action still more lively. Every accent of his voice spoke to the ear; every feature of his face, and every motion of his hands spoke to the eye. The most dissipated and thoughtless found their attention involuntarily fixed; and the dullest and most ignorant could not but understand. Had his natural talents for oratory been employed in secular affairs, and been somewhat more improved by refinements of art and embellishments of erudition, it is possible they would soon have advanced him to distinguished wealth and renown.

"But not to dwell longer on his accomplishments as an orator, one thing remains to be mentioned of an infinitely higher order, namely, the power of God, which so remarkably accompanied his labours. It is here Mr. Whitefield is most to be envied." [24]

We should not be carried away by an admiration of Whitefield's natural

11

gifts. A burning heart empowered by the Spirit of God and a soul possessed by the Lord Jesus Christ formed the basis from which the messages came. On occasion Whitefield would kneel in prayer before preaching, agonising audibly for the souls who were before him, then before rising would continue on his knees for a long time in the most profound silence—a stillness like that of the tomb pervading the whole place.

According to an intimate friend, Cornelius Winter, Whitefield, in later life, sometimes, towards the end of his sermons, would don a judge's cap, and with profound solemnity enact, and pronounce, the words of Christ: "Depart from me ye cursed into everlasting fire prepared for the devil and his angels". As can be imagined the effect of this was overwhelming. What can preachers today learn from the example of the great preacher of the 18th century? His extraordinary gifts do not assist those of limited ability, but the following observations could prove helpful.

1. *Simplicity of Structure*
Whitefield's custom was to use three or four points. That he sometimes followed Matthew Henry is evident. The use of a simple outline containing the main thrust of the Gospel message is of help, not only to the congregation but also to the preacher himself.

2. *Doctrinal Content*
Ryle declares that Whitefield preached a "singularly pure Gospel". He never neglected the great themes of total depravity, the new birth, justification by faith, the atonement and the judgment to come. He did not hesitate to describe the torments of the damned. The love of God was apparent not only in the words preached but in his own demeanour and often in his tears.

3. *Specific Pointed Application Throughout*
The sermons were aimed at the conscience and application was not left to the final few minutes. The place of the moral law and its meaning for every day life is apparent in the outlines that have been left for us. It ought to be stressed that the sermon material that has been published is very inadequate as far as gaining a right impression of Whitefield's preaching is concerned. This is not only because of inadequate and limited records but also because cold print cannot do justice to the pathos or gesture employed in powerful preaching.

4. *A Suitable Use of Illustration*
Whitefield's use of simile, metaphor and anecdote brought colour, life and movement to his sermons. His extraordinary power of description turned ears into eyes.

5. *Flexibility*

Whitefield was able to adapt himself to the various situations with which he was confronted. Not all his sermons were models of systematic arrangement. A theological professor from America who heard him once in London declared of the sermon that "It was not very orderly but did more good than all the other sermons I heard".[25] It is possible for a preacher to be so concerned about method that he is not in a position to view a situation in perspective and so present the most relevant material for the occasion. Better a relevant message, suitable at a certain time, than a brilliant orderly exposition which is irrelevant to a particular need.

To illustrate the primacy of preaching in the life of Whitefield, one could turn to the distressing circumstances in which he found himself upon his return from America in 1741, after 18 months of absence. Whitefield did not concern himself with organisation as much as John Wesley. Too much has been made of Whitefield's lack of organisational ability. There is evidence everywhere in his life of tremendous strength in the realm of making plans and organising their execution. He was a pioneer *par excellence*. The fact that he did not choose to organise a new denomination does not reflect on his organisational abilities. At this time he was in debt to the extent of £1,000 (a large sum in those days). He was threatened with arrest for a debt of £350. He found himself utterly rejected by the establishment, especially for criticising a certain Bishop Tillotson. His work was divided at Bristol, Cennick contending for particular redemption and the Wesleys for general redemption. Wesley had attacked him because of his belief in predestination. Many converts in London disdained him on account of the predestination controversy. He felt acute disappointment at this rejection by some of his own converts. He grieved particularly over the division at Bristol, especially since he was the pioneer of that work.

With burdens that would sink an average man in a sea of despondency Whitefield proceeded to wield the outstanding gift with which God had endued him. He gave himself to preaching. Such was the response in his first visit to Scotland following his return from America in 1741 that the debts were soon paid. He then returned to London to make a spiritual assault upon Moorfields. Tyerman gives the following description of this attack which began on a Monday:

"Being thus encouraged, I ventured out again at noon: but what a scene! The fields, the whole fields, seemed, in a bad sense of the word, all white, ready, not for the Redeemer's, but, for Beelzebub's harvest. All his agents were in full motion, drummers, trumpeters, merry-andrews, masters of puppet-shows, exhibitors of wild beasts, etc.—all busy in entertaining their respective auditories. I suppose, there could not be less than 20,000 or 30,000 people.

"My pulpit was fixed on the opposite side, and immediately, to their great mortification, they found the number of their attendants sadly lessened. Judging that, like St. Paul, I should now be called, as it were, to fight with beasts at Ephesus, I preached from these words: 'Great is Diana of the Ephesians'. You may easily guess, that there was some noise among the craftsmen, and that I was honoured with having stones, dirt, rotten eggs, and pieces of dead cats thrown at me, whilst engaged in calling them from their favourite, but lying vanities. My soul was indeed among lions; but far the greater part of my congregation seemed to be turned into lambs.

"This encouraged me to give notice, that I would preach again at six o'clock in the evening. I came, I saw, but what? Thousands and thousands more than before, still more deeply engaged in their unhappy diversions; but, among them, some thousands waiting as earnestly to hear the Gospel. This was what Satan could not brook. One of his choicest servants was exhibiting, trumpeting on a large stage; but, as soon as the people saw me, in my black robes, and my pulpit, I think all of them, to a man, left him and ran to me. For a while I was enabled to lift up my voice as a trumpet. God's people kept praying; and the enemy's agents made a kind of roaring at some distance from us. At length, they approached nearer, and the merry-andrew (who complained that they had taken many pounds less that day on account of my preaching) got upon a man's shoulders, and advancing near the pulpit, attempted, several times to strike me with a long, heavy whip; but always, with the violence of his motion, tumbled down. Soon afterwards, they got a recruiting sergeant, with his drum, etc., to pass through the congregation. I gave the word of command, and ordered that way might be made for the king's officer. The ranks opened, while all marched quietly through, and then closed again. Finding those efforts to fail, a large body, on the opposite side of the field, assembled together, and, having got a large pole for their standard, advanced towards us with steady and formidable steps, till they came very near the skirts of our congregation. I saw, gave warning, and prayed to the Captain of our salvation for support and deliverance. He heard and answered; for, just as they approached us, with looks full of resentment, they quarrelled among themselves, threw down their pole, and went their way, leaving, however, many of their company behind. I think I continued in praying, preaching and singing (for the noise, at times, was too great to preach), about three hours.

"We then retired to the Tabernacle. My pocket was full of notes from persons brought under concern. I read them amidst the praises and spiritual acclamations of thousands, who joined with the holy angels in rejoicing that so many sinners were snatched, in such unlikely place and manner, out of the very jaws of the devil. This was the beginning of the Tabernacle Society. Three hundred and fifty awakened souls were

14

received in one day; and, I believe, the number of notes (messages) exceeded a thousand." [26]

The battle raged until Wednesday and it was at this time that Whitefield narrowly escaped with his life when an attempt was made to stab him. It would seem that the preaching was of such order that little children were drawn as well as adults. Concerning this episode at Moorfields, Whitefield wrote:

"I cannot help adding, that, several little boys and girls were fond of sitting round me on the pulpit, while I preached, and handing to me the people's notes. Though they were often struck with the eggs, dirt, etc., thrown at me, they never once gave way; but, on the contrary, every time I was struck, turned up their little weeping eyes, and seemed to wish they could receive the blows for me." [27]

3. The importance of the doctrines of grace

Before considering Whitefield's experience of free grace we ought not to assume that the terminology used is understood. There is need to be explicit as to what is meant by "the doctrines of grace".

When the Scriptures declare that we are "justified *freely* by His *grace*" [28] the *freely* means that nothing is required of man in order to merit his justification by way of price or satisfaction. There is no prerequisite or preparatory disposition required to merit salvation. If God foresees anything in a man to make him more fit for salvation than his neighbour, then the question of merit arises. If that be the case, grace ceases to be grace. The term *grace* should be adequate in itself but the word *freely* doubles the emphasis, so as to exclude, in the absolute sense, anything whatsoever in the realm of human merit.

Faith, however, is thought by many to be exceptional and fall outside the category of merit. In other words it is widely held that God foresaw all who would believe and thus was obliged to constitute them heirs of salvation. The notion of free will is essential to support this theory. All are free to believe. Some do, some do not. Hence the reason why some are saved. So runs the popular idea. But Paul expressly denies this scheme of things when he declares, "Therefore it is of faith, that it might be of grace".[29] Faith is the means or instrument by which the sinner is united to Christ. Faith is not the meritorious cause. Christ is our merit. Faith is the gift of God.[30] In no other way then, could salvation be by grace, except through the gift of grace, which is faith.

Grace is not only termed "free" it is also sometimes described as "sovereign".[31] Sovereign grace implies that the choice lies with God Himself.[32] By nature all mankind reject God, Christ and the Gospel. If God chooses some to be redeemed by a mighty work of regeneration stemming from Christ then that is gracious. God is not obliged to save those who hate him.

This was the issue which was already beginning to divide Wesley and his disciples from Whitefield and his helpers in 1739 when Whitefield came, as we shall see, to grasp these matters with a firmer understanding. But to sum up "the doctrines of grace" the matter can be stated as follows. Man's will is enslaved. He is unable to contribute anything towards salvation. God has chosen those whom He will save. He does this by regeneration. (Some call this irresistible grace.) For the elect God has given Christ as an atoning sacrifice. In addition to this He has given the gift of the Holy Spirit to ensure that what is begun in regeneration, will be completed in sanctification which means that those regenerated will persevere to the end.

Since the Reformers taught these things from Scripture the term "Reformed Faith" is sometimes used. The Puritans specialised in the exposition of Scripture and continued and developed the teachings of the Reformers. Hence the general use of the term "Puritanism". "Calvinism" is a word frequently used to describe the "doctrines of grace". We need to remember, however, that in many quarters enemies of truth have misrepresented the words "Calvinism", and "Puritanism" with caricatures by which these terms have been horribly distorted. Care needs to be exercised, therefore, in regard to their use.

Whitefield had already imbibed the elements of Calvinism by reading Puritan books. His experience of grace in conversion was deep and in the course of his ministerial duties he became conversant with the doctrines. However, the profound significance of these issues was indelibly impressed upon him in 1739 at the age of 24. During the voyage taking him to America for the second time he was overwhelmed by a deep conviction of sin. Marvellous things had been witnessed by him during the previous six months. Hundreds, perhaps thousands, had been converted through his preaching during that time.[33] For a minister so young the temptation to pride was as wide as the ocean which surrounded him during the eleven-week journey.

He was to be preserved from that sin, however, by means of a special work of the Holy Spirit in leading him more deeply into what he himself described as "The mystery of His electing, soul transforming love".[34] That he should be saved at all became a source of amazement. This experience is described in different ways in Scripture. Daniel spoke of, "confusion of face"[35] and when he was given a vision of Christ he declared, "and there remained no strength in me: for my comeliness was turned in me into corruption".[36]   Isaiah when confronted with the glory of Jehovah felt acutely the uncleanness of his lips.[37]   Job at the end of a long chastisement repented and abhorred himself in dust and ashes.[38] Paul cried out, "O wretched man that I am!"[39]   It seems that every truly great man of God is made outstandingly fruitful through first being humbled and made little in his own sight.   Every preacher of repentance must first know the plague of his own heart before he can be effective in exposing to others the native depravity of their own hearts.   Having experienced every note and chord on the keyboard of Godly sorrow[40] he will be apt in the proclamation of repentance to others.

Surely the whole business of salvation concerns the destruction of man's pride and self-sufficiency.   All that exalts man has to be brought down. What is the world about, but daily to promote human reason and exalt man's wisdom?   Every mortal goes about to establish his own little tower of Babel from which to pipe his own song of self-sufficiency.   All men, unless changed by grace, are swift to proclaim the adequacy of their own goodness.   What is the use then of a preacher unless he has come to experience, and that in a very vivid way, the total destruction of self-righteousness and the demolition of every pretension of self-merit before God.   The unconverted cannot fathom these convictions of the godly for their whole philosophy and outlook is otherwise orientated.   The trumpet sounds of Whitefield's preaching which brought down the walls of so many Jerichos in the souls of men can be traced to his own experience of humiliation and repentance before God.

Regarding this time Whitefield wrote in his journals:
"A sense of my actual sins and natural deformity humbled me exceedingly;   and then the freeness and riches of God's everlasting love broke in with such light and power upon my soul, that I was often awed into silence and could not speak.[41]

"I underwent inexpressible agonies of soul for two or three days, at the remembrance of my sins and the bitter consequences of them.   All the while I was assured that God had forgiven me, but I could not forgive myself for sinning against so much light and love.   I felt something of that which . . . Peter (felt) when, with oaths and curses he had thrice denied his Master.   At length my Lord looked upon me, and with that look broke my rocky heart, and I wept most bitterly . . . Were I always to see myself such a sinner as I am, and as I did then, without seeing the Saviour of sinners, I should not be able to look up."[42]

Arnold Dallimore comments upon these quotations as follows:
Whitefield's whole outlook, both theological and in relationship to the daily Christian life, was affected by this deeper understanding of Divine grace.   In his letters he began to tell forth the truths he had thus experi-

enced and, in so doing, enunciated the basic tenets of a theological system —the system which is known as Calvinism.[43]

It can be seen then that the young evangelist did not learn grace merely out of books, important as they may be. During the voyage he read works by Jenks, Hammond, Thomas Boston (The Fourfold State), Ralph Erskine and John Edwards.[44]

Conviction of sin in the heart is the key to understanding the meaning of God's grace. Some stop with a head knowledge of doctrine. Intellectual knowledge is not to be despised, but better for the truth to be written within. A man who loves the doctrines of grace is a man who shows a double work of the Spirit. Not only has he been saved by the Holy Spirit's work, but he has come by the same Spirit to a joyful appreciation of the stupendous significance of his salvation.

Whitefield was stedfast in his insistence that what he believed was Biblical. On arrival in America he said, "My doctrine I had from Jesus Christ and His Apostles: I was taught them by God".[45]

During the voyage he wrote to his friend James Hervey:

It is sweet to know and preach that Christ justifies the ungodly, and that all truly good works are not so much as partly the cause, but the effect of our justification before God. Till convinced of these truths you must own free will in man, which is directly contrary to the Holy Scriptures and the articles of our church. Let me advise dear Mr. H., laying aside all prejudice, to read and pray over St. Paul's epistles to the Romans and Galatians, and then let him tell me what he thinks of this doctrine.[46]

David of old slew Goliath with one stone. He did not need the other four although their presence must have been a comfort to him. The doctrines of grace are sometimes classified under five points,[47] but it is a heart experience of the first one, total depravity, which brings down the giant of man's pride and lays that Goliath in the dust. Once let a man know how vile he is before a holy God and he will be ready to receive God's way of salvation. Conviction of sin in the soul is like John the Baptist crying, "Prepare ye the way of the Lord, make his paths straight". Whitefield's experience in 1739 made the way level for the doctrines of free grace to live richly in his heart and shine gloriously in his ministry.

Those who deride the Reformed faith and maintain that it is detrimental to evangelism must account for a man like Whitefield. He believed in unconditional election and the bondage of man's will, yet none so freely invited sinners to Jesus Christ. He stressed the absolute lostness and inability of man to save himself. At the same time he upheld the absolute sovereign power of God to save. Upon this basis he exposed his hearers to the reality of their appalling condition and brought them to an end of all confidence in their own ability. At the same time he pictured the omnipotence of God and directed the helpless to call upon the only source of help.

The importance of the doctrines of grace for today can be seen in the fact that God is frequently dishonoured as helpless to save men until they declare their willingness to allow Him to do so. Thus the ability of man is stressed alongside God's inability.

Finally, we should remember the foremost place of repentance in the Gospel message. Repentance is "an evangelical grace". In other words, God gives repentance. This is not to say that man is not responsible to repent. When Adam fell he lost his ability to please God, "they that are in the flesh cannot please God". But he did not lose his responsibility to keep and fulfill every aspect of the moral law. When the doctrines of grace are preached it is shown that man is totally responsible to meet all the requirements, including the spiritual requirements, of the moral law, yet at the same time he has lost all ability to do so. Thus the terrifying predicament of man is highlighted. He is responsible to repent and to have a change of heart but, at the same time, he is destitute of the ability to will and to do God's good pleasure. Simultaneously, he is pointed toward, and closed up to, a sovereign God upon whom he is compelled to call for mercy and salvation.

Those who come to believe the doctrines of grace as Whitefield believed them, are obligated at the same time to show the same fervour and compassion for the souls of men as he did, lest it be concluded (and that with some justification) that their faith is merely intellectual. It may be said that in Whitefield we find an excellent exemplification of doctrine combined with practice.

In his preaching, the sovereign election of the Father was placed alongside the free invitations to come to the Saviour, who Himself declared, "All that the Father giveth me will come unto me, and him that cometh unto me I will in no wise cast out".[48]

In 1741, returning to England, he wrote to one of his friends, "May you live to see the spirit of Scriptural Puritanism universally prevail".[49] That Whitefield loved the doctrines of the Puritans to the end is seen by a statement he made three years before his death when speaking of the Puritans in a preface to the republication of John Bunyan's complete works, "Though dead, by their writings they yet speak. A peculiar unction attends them to this very hour".[50]

It is interesting to note that Spurgeon expresses the same convictions a century later. Writing to his friends from Mentone, in 1882, he declared, "My life is dedicated to the proclamation of the everlasting Gospel of the grace of God: pray that the truth may be mighty and prevail among all classes of the community. Puritanism has been spoken of with a sneer; may we live to see it the leading power in Christendom. The doctrines of grace shall come to the front again if only we exhibit the grace of the doctrine".[51]

No greater blessing could come to the world today than a revival of Puritanism, for therein we are brought face to face with essential, but neglected, truths, such as the moral law and repentance. When the Holy Spirit anoints men, as He did Whitefield, "to exhibit the grace of the doctrine", we can be sure that, "the parched ground shall become a pool, and the thirsty land springs of water".[52]

BIBLIOGRAPHY

For those who have never read anything about George Whitefield, *The Select Sermons,* including a 46 pp. biography by J. C. Ryle, is ideal. This is published as a paperback by The Banner of Truth Trust. Volume 1 of Whitefield's life by Arnold Dallimore, also by The Banner of Truth Trust, is most readable and enjoyable. The latter traces Whitefield's career up to 1740 when he was 25 years of age. Other biographies are occasionally available on the second-hand book market, such as that by Robert Philip (605 pp.). The latter is disappointing. For the student the work by Whitefield's contemporary, Gillies, *Memoirs of the Life of the Reverend George Whitefield* (135 pp., 1772) and the two volumes by Luke Tyerman (561 and 642 pp., 1876) and the aforementioned biography by Dallimore (598 pp.) are very important, as is of course, *Whitefield's Journals* (594 pp.) republished by The Banner of Truth Trust in 1960. The author was privileged to have a part in preparing the latter for publication and can testify to the correctness of Spurgeon's judgment that while "other men seem to be only half alive—Whitefield was all life, fire, wing, force". Whitefield's works published in six volumes (three of which contain nearly 1,500 letters) were published in 1771. These volumes were edited inadequately and their resurrection by way of worthy attention and attractive republication is awaited still.

REFERENCES

1. *George Whitefield.* Arnold Dallimore, p. 5. Banner of Truth Trust, 1970 (hereafter referred to as *Dallimore's Whitefield*). 2. *Select Sermons of Whitefield,* intro. by Ryle, p. 27. 3. *Dallimore's Whitefield,* p. 6. 4. *Whitefield's Journals,* Introduction. 5. One of Spurgeon's notable lectures was "Seraphic Zeal, as exhibited in the Life of Whitefield". cf. Spurgeon's autobiography, Vol. 3, p. 45. 6. *Select Sermons.* Intro. by Ryle, p. 16. 7. *ibid.,* p. 16. Ryle is mistaken as to the source of this information. It is not in *The Journals,* but found in one of Whitefield's letters. cf. *Tyerman,* Vol. 1, p. 50. 8. *ibid.,* p. 17. 9. *Tyerman,* Vol. 1, p. 64.

10. After more than 20 years of specialised study of this period Arnold Dallimore contends, in correspondence with the writer, that revival followed the evangelist's ministry up until his death in 1770. 11. *Gillies, Memoirs of Whitefield*, p. 5. 12. *Tyerman*, Vol. 2, p. 626. 13. *Tyerman*, Vol. 1, p. 509. 14. Matt. 24:5. 15. *Dallimore's Whitefield*, p. 25. 16. *Journals*, p. 267. 17. *ibid.*, pp. 262, 265, 277. 18. *Dallimore's Whitefield*, p. 264. 19. *Tyerman*, Vol. 1, p. 376. 20. *George Whitefield's Works*, p. 405. A detailed account of the revival and its lasting effects is provided by A. Fawcett in *The Cambuslang Revival*, Banner of Truth Trust. 21. *Tyerman*, Vol. 2, p. 5. 22. *Tyerman*, Vol. 2, p. 625. 23. *Dallimore's Whitefield*, p. 539. 24. *Tyerman*, Vol. 12, p. 628. 25. *Tyerman*, Vol. 2, p. 324. 26. *Tyerman*, Vol. 1, p. 555. 27. *ibid.*, p. 557 See also *George Whitefield Works*, Vol. 1, pp. 250-270. 28. Rom. 3: 24. 29. Rom. 4: 16. 30. Eph. 2: 8, 9; II Pet. 1: 1; Heb. 12: 2. 31. Rom. ch. 9. 32. John 15: 16. 33. *Tyerman*, Vol. 1, p. 307. 34. *Works*, Vol. 1, p. 92. 35. Dan. 9: 7. 36. Dan. 10: 8. 37. Isa. 6: 5. 38. Job 42: 6. 39. Rom. 7: 24. 40. 2 Cor. 7: 10. 41. *Journals*, p. 331. 42. *ibid.*, p. 334. 43. *Dallimore's Whitefield*, p. 404. 44. John Edwards is not to be confused with Jonathan Edwards with whom Whitefield was shortly to have fellowship. 45. *Works*, Vol. 1, p. 98. 46. *ibid.*, p. 95. 47. (1) Total depravity; (2) Unconditional election; (3) Limited atonement; (4) Irresistible grace; (5) Perseverence of the saints. 48. John 6: 37. 49. *Tyerman*, Vol. 1, p. 459. 50. *Tyerman*, Vol. 2, p. 508. 51. *Metropolitan Tabernacle Pulpit*, Vol. 28, p. 648. 52. Isa. 35: 7.

FREE WILL OR GOD'S GRACE?

LUTHER'S REFORMATION CONFLICT WITH ERASMUS

Jim van Zyl

IN RECENT YEARS A RENEWED INTEREST IN THE REFORMERS AND THE Puritans has swelled to large proportions. Published works have multiplied, with the result that distorted ideas of the Puritans have, to a large extent, been dispelled. Yet vital areas remain. One of these concerns the will. In order to grapple with this it is fitting that we should take a look at a particular aspect of Luther's teaching which is more often than not overlooked, namely, his conflict with Erasmus over the question of the will of the sinner.

Luther himself considered this issue as absolutely crucial to the concept of grace in the gospel. Writing to Erasmus in December 1525 in his book "De Servo Arbitrio"—"On the Enslaved Will"—he says: 'You alone have attacked the real thing, that is, the essential issue. You have not worried me with those extraneous issues about the Papacy, purgatory, indulgences and the like—trifles, rather than issues . . . you, and you alone, have seen the hinge on which all turns, and aimed for the vital spot. For that I heartily thank you . . ." (p. 319). Luther never considered this a merely academic issue. As Dr. J. I. Packer and O. R. Johnston write in the preface to their new translation of Luther's great work: " 'Free-will' was no academic question to Luther; the whole gospel of the grace of God, he held, was bound up with it, and stood or fell according to the way one decided it. In 'The Bondage of the Will', therefore, Luther believes himself to be fighting for the truth of God, the only hope of man; and . . . his conviction that the faith once delivered to the saints, and in consequence the salvation of precious souls, is here at stake" (p. 42).

We must ask ourselves whether in fact Luther was correct here! Is the Gospel at stake at this point? Does this question involve precious souls and their eternal destiny?

Whatever mistakes the Reformers made, they were unquestionably men with an immense concept of the Gospel; a thorough grasp of biblical doctrine and a deep sense of responsibility towards lost sinners.

While they were men of deep learning (most of them University trained), they did not bring about far-reaching changes in European history and Church history by a cool, detached outlook. They did not hand down instructions from ivory towers. No. They were men of action; immersed in warfare and covered with the dust of battle. They fought constantly for the life of the Church and the truth of the Gospel. But to return to the question of free-will, it is surely significant that all the leading Reformers considered this question a crucial one—Luther, Calvin, Knox, Zwingli, Bucer, Huss, Farel, Wycliffe, Wishart, Bradford, Jerome of Prague and a host of others. Rather than dismissing these men as primitive, does it not behove us to ask ourselves whether perhaps *we* have watered down the Gospel? Have we really pondered the sinfulness of sin? Have we examined the outcome of the catastrophic consequences of Adam's fall? Have we faced up to the implications of original sin and depravity? And have we formulated Scriptural views of God's grace?

It will not be possible to deal with every aspect of Luther's and Erasmus's writings and their views and arguments. We have only time to place their conflict in its historical background—highlight some of the main arguments—and seek to evaluate the whole from a biblical point of view. I think it is also very important to realise at the outset that the question of "Free-will" *is in fact* beset with problems. It would be foolish in the extreme to treat this subject in a cavalier manner, or give the impression that it is all really very simple and easy. It is nothing of the kind. There are some knots which even Bishop J. C. Ryle could not untie! But this does not mean that we can contract out of the debate.

Most major Christian doctrines are beset with inscrutable aspects but we hold to them none the less! The Virgin Birth, the Trinity, the Inspiration of Scriptures and Eternal Security all involve deep problems. But an evangelical should never say: "I cannot present this to the world, or proclaim this because I cannot square it all up". We do not entirely comprehend all that we believe but that does not preclude our proclaiming the Gospel.

Erasmus

Desiderius Erasmus was born in Rotterdam between 1466 and 1469, the illegitimate son of a priest and a physician's daughter. He quickly showed himself to be a prodigy at the famous school at Deventer which was run by the Brethren of the Common Life. It was probably here that he picked up his enthusiasm for biblical studies and a kind of mystical piety as distinct from Evangelical piety. After this, he went to the monastery of Steyn in 1486 where he cultivated his strong love for classical literature and thought. Interestingly enough, the monastery was of the Augustinian Order to which Luther had also belonged. After seven years he there obtained a dispensation of temporary leave and, after spending a year or two as secretary to the Bishop of Cambrai, he went to Paris. His Order was never able to reclaim him.

His experiences while studying in Paris for a doctorate in theology were disappointing. The teaching was stern, inhuman and an affront to a tender and sensitive soul like Erasmus. After this followed a series of visits to England punctuated by returns to the Continent. In England he met the fiery Colet and became firm friends of Sir Thomas More and other Englishmen who were leaders in the English Humanistic movement. His visits only spurred on his studies in the classics and, in particular, Greek.

A child of the Renaissance (to which we will refer again in a moment), Erasmus sought to turn Renaissance learning to the service of religion. He conceived the plan of publishing the writings of the early Fathers and the biblical text itself. By 1500 he was already working towards a new

25

Greek edition of the New Testament to replace the imperfect Latin Vulgate editions. This, he hoped, would spur on a new Reformation within Christendom which would recapture the pristine purity of apostolic Christianity. It is important however, as we shall see, that his concept of "A Reformation" and of "New Testament Christianity" was very far removed from that of Luther's.

Erasmus's Greek New Testament edition appeared for the first time in 1516, a work that was by no means perfect. It was marred by typographical errors, and for the most part was based on only four manuscripts. These did not supply the last six verses of Revelation, and so Erasmus obligingly supplied his own Greek rendering by translating from the Latin Vulgate. The fifth edition appeared in 1536. This work by a Humanist scholar became a mighty weapon in the hand of the Reformers! We can see clearly the providential and sovereign Hand of God in supplying the Scriptures without which there could be no Reformation. Erasmus was anxious that all people should be allowed to read the New Testament in the vernacular. Listen to his eloquent plea: "I wish that even the most humble women should read the Gospel and the Epistles of St. Paul. And these should also be translated into every tongue, so that they might be read and known not only by the Scots and Irish, but also by the Turks and Saracens . . . Would that the ploughboy recited something from them at his plough, and the weaver sang from them at his loom, and the traveller whiled away the tedium of his journey with their tales, indeed, that the speech of Christian men were drawn from them".

On the Continent he became foremost in the Renaissance and Humanist movement as he stayed at Ghent, Antwerp, Louvain, Liege, Mainz and Strasbourg. Finally he settled at Basle. A stream of writings came from his pen and he was acknowledged as unsurpassed in his field of scholarship.

Important factors must be kept in mind if we are to understand the conflict between Erasmus and Luther.

Erasmus grew up north of the Alps, where Humanism often sought for itself a religious or Christian guise or framework. The Renaissance in Italy gave rise directly to non-Christian and even anti-Christian ideals, views and scholarships; it provided little moral restraint and in essence was "permissive". North of the Alps, however, in the Netherlands and Germany for example, the Renaissance had stronger ties with religion and morality. It was as V. H. H. Green says: ". . . . an 'intellectual revolution with religious overtones'". It was within this framework that Erasmus grew up and strove to rediscover the original texts of the Scriptures and the early Church Fathers in order to return to the values of the early Church. He mercilessly exposed the mumbo-jumbo of the Roman Catholic Church. While he poured ridicule and sarcasm upon the priests and their hypocrisy, he himself was not sceptical about religion. By contrast, the Renaissance scholars in the south of Europe were highly sceptical (men like Bracciolini, the licentious collector of ancient manuscripts; the wealthy Florentine families; Lorenzo Valla who advocated a life of freedom in every sphere including morality; the Renaissance popes embodied in Julius II).

Erasmus, essentially a Renaissance thinker and scholar, and a man deeply imbibed with the spirit of Humanism drawn largely from the Greek philosophers, mixed Greek philosophy with Christian religion. The synthesis which resulted was not to Luther's taste.

Not surprisingly Erasmus laid great stress on Man's Reason and ability to know and gain mastery over himself; indeed to contribute something towards his own salvation. He could never bring himself to a view of man as a totally fallen creature altogether in need of God's grace. As James Atkinson says: "In a paradoxical way his very goodness and decency and refinement served to put him beyond the reach of the Gospel. Erasmus could be improved but hardly needed redemption".

Later, as we hear his arguments, we must always keep this in mind.

Then we need to observe that Erasmus scorned Doctrine. Theology did not interest him—and this becomes evident in his clash with Luther. He had been sickened by the barren intellectualism of Aquinas and Scotus the schoolmen, and erroneously jumped to the conclusion that the Reformers were likewise barren dogmatists intent upon splitting hairs over unimportant doctrinal points. Clarity in biblical doctrine, he believed, led to the killing of the spiritual life.

Thus Erasmus propagated a mystical piety based upon a supposed "simple religion" found in the New Testament. He emphasised practical Christian living and emphasised following the example of Christ and the early disciples.

From all this we can see that Erasmus had an inadequate concept of sin, both doctrinally and experimentally. He refused to take the biblical teaching to its logical conclusion for this affronted his humanistic bias. He never underwent the intense conviction and torment and soul-struggle that Luther experienced. This was utterly foreign to him. He was superficial, both in doctrine and experience. He was, to quote J. I. Packer and O. R. Johnston, ". . . shrewd but shallow, a man of cool calculation rather than of burning conviction" (p. 19). This together with a temperament that loathed controversy and debate; that longed for the peace of the study; that revelled in the new culture of learning and sophistication and prized peace rather than the truth will help us to understand why, despite all his brilliance and gifts, Erasmus can never be placed alongside the Reformers, either in regard to suffering for the Gospel or accomplishment in regard to the reformation of the Church.

As we shall see, an inadequate view of sin led Erasmus to an unscriptural concept of God's grace. These issues lie at the very heart of the Gospel and so Erasmus's whole system of thought was undermined.

Luther

A detailed history of Luther's life is unnecessary since most of us know the facts. He was fourteen years younger than Erasmus and, by the time he began lecturing at the University of Wittenberg as Professor of Theology in 1513, he was a first-class scholar. Commencing his studies in law, he later changed to theology. In 1505, at the age of 22, he entered an Augustinian monastery at Erfurt. By this time he was already deeply involved in seeking for peace with God. The awful sense of the majesty and holiness of God overwhelmed him as early as 1507 and was always present in his approach to theology.

Luther suffered the most intense pangs of conviction of his own sinfulness and asked the question: "Have I fasted, watched, prayed, confessed enough?"

His studies did not help him, for they were based on the current Nomalist views based on the work of Occam. Occam taught that man could, by his own free-will unaided by grace, choose to do what was morally good and avoid what was morally bad; that man could through his own powers love God above all things. This Luther knew from profound and bitter experience to be destitute of truth. He knew his own heart too well!

The light seems to have broken through to him while lecturing on the Psalms as new Professor at Wittenberg. He says: "When I became a Doctor, I did not yet know that we cannot expiate our sins". But at some point (the exact date will probably never be known) he discovered the glorious truth of the righteousness of God that is freely available to us through faith in Christ! He had discovered the truth of free grace!

Thus, in vivid contrast to Erasmus, the dispassionate scholar aloof and remote, and despising doctrine, Luther was cast headlong into an experience in which he came to know at first hand the sinfulness of sin, and a

28

consequent search for clear truth which would spell out salvation in precise terms.

The two men came from similar academic backgrounds, but were very different in their approach to, understanding and grasp of biblical doctrine. This difference was peculiarly marked in their individual spiritual experience.

Under these circumstances it is not surprising that the two men finally clashed head-on. Initially there was speculation that the two would join forces. In 1518 Erasmus could still affirm in a general way in his correspondence that Luther had said and done much that was good. About Luther's doctrinal views on certain subjects Erasmus was diplomatically vague. By 1519 their rapprochement was probably as close as it ever could be.

Erasmus, however, had enemies because of his exposure of malpractices within the Roman Catholic Church. Dominican and Carmelite monks at Louvain began to spread rumours that Erasmus had actually helped Luther write some of his heresies! Luther himself wrote to Erasmus on March 28, 1519, asking for support.

Clearly Erasmus was put on a spot. He had enough discernment to see that if he were to side with Luther, he would immediately be plunged headlong into the fierce battle that was then rending Europe. This was too much for him. He was a peaceable man. He hated controversy. For some time Erasmus remained in a state of indecision. Very guardedly he would speak generously about Luther. But always he left the way open for retreat. Writing to the Archbishop of Mainz, Erasmus showed caution. "I do not know him; I have only had time to glance at his books; I have advised him to be moderate; I am neither his patron nor his accuser."

The year 1520 was decisive. Luther broke finally with Rome in person and print, while Erasmus came to see how deeply he in turn was separated from Luther. In September 1520 Erasmus—now in a tone quite different from his letter to the Archbishop of Mainz—wrote to the Pope disclaiming any connection with Luther. By 1523 the pressures on Erasmus had become intolerable. No less a person than the King of England urged him to write against Luther.

At last in September 1524 there appeared his diatribe on the Free-will— "Discussion or Collation, concerning Free-will". Conscious of the step he had taken he wrote on September 6 to Henry VIII: "The die is cast. The little book on free-will has seen the light of day". It is beyond reasonable doubt that Erasmus wrote the book under pressure, but the views expressed were his own.

Luther did not reply immediately. A full year passed before his answer finally appeared, nl. "De Servo Arbitrio" (On the Enslaved Will). It was four times longer than Erasmus's work, strongly controversial, considerably blunter and containing a thorough exegesis of key passages of Scripture. It was probably more significant than most people realised at the time that when Erasmus did finally choose to attack Luther he did so at this particular point! He might have chosen one of a dozen other topics, but Erasmus had the insight to see exactly where the ultimate difference lay in their concept of sin and grace.

I will deal with four main areas of disagreement.

Four main points

(a) *The importance of the problem of " Free-will " in itself.*

Erasmus maintained that free-will was among the "useless doctrines that we can do without". It was ". . . irreligious, idle, superfluous". It was quite unnecessary to delve into such a subject which was not a central doctrine of the Christian faith. It could be quite easily avoided without watering down Christianity. Luther replied that in actual fact it *is* vital for us to know precisely what ability free-will has because it involves our salvation. Ignorance on this score will lead to ignorance of God's part in salvation, and this again to ignorance about our whole relationship to God. Thus we will not be able to . . . "worship, praise, give thanks or serve Him, for we do not know how much we should attribute to ourselves and how much to Him. We need, therefore, to have in mind a clear-cut distinction between God's power and ours, and God's work and ours, if we would live a godly life".

It is also important to have an accurate picture of what free-will really is, because it involves the whole Christian life. Nothing could be more enervating and calculated to bring spiritual depression than the teaching that God's will can be frustrated at certain points by my so-called free-will. This immediately opens the door to chance, luck and uncertainty.

(b) *Definition of Free-will.*

It is obvious that this area was crucial and we must give our close attention to it. In typical fashion, Erasmus expressed himself in more than one way in defining free-will.

At one stage Erasmus says that ". . . the human will after sin is so depraved that it has lost its freedom and is forced to serve sin, and cannot recall itself to a better state". Then he says in the same vein: "As in those who lack grace (special grace, I mean) reason is darkened but not destroyed, so that it is probable that their power of will is not wholly destroyed, but has become ineffective for upright actions". Finally he says, seemingly striking into a different direction altogether: "Moreover, I conceive of 'free-will' in this context as a power of the human will by which a man may apply himself to those things that lead to eternal salvation, or turn away from the same". This latter definition was the one that Erasmus worked out with the greatest consistency and taking the overall picture is the one which more nearly expresses his belief than any other.

Erasmus, therefore, maintained that the will of the sinner has an inherent power to move itself either in the direction of God and his salvation, or else to reject the same. Sin has undoubtedly affected it but certainly not paralysed it.

Indeed Erasmus not only held that man's will had only been *weakened* by sin, but that it was still capable of meritorious action, *i.e.* actions capable of gaining spiritual merit in God's sight. He admitted that this power of the human will is only a very little power, but maintained that it is power nonetheless, and even though it gains only a very little merit, it still gains genuine merit! Thus he still stood shrouded in the death-clothes of both Greek philosophy and Roman Catholicism. It is by this meritorious application to spiritual truths that salvation is ultimately secured.

Now, according to Erasmus, what connection was there between free-will, merit, spiritual truths and salvation? First of all, the sinner has the power to make himself fit for the gift of internal grace. In other words, he could remove the barrier which had hitherto stood in the way of God's giving; he could turn to God; he could take the first step. This was so-called *Congruent merit*. God was not obliged to respond in any way, but in actual fact He did by giving to the sinner internal grace.

Once this grace (or supernatural spiritual energy) had been given, the sinner could use it for works of a quality of goodness previously out of his reach. Now the more good works he did the more it placed God under an obligation—to give even more grace to the sinner, this was called *Condign merit*, and ultimately it placed God under the obligation to grant the sinner heavenly glory.

Thus the sinner not only takes the first step towards God, but ultimately places God under an obligation to grant him entrance into heaven. Erasmus attempted to wriggle out of the idea of Obligation by maintaining that Congruent merit resulted in God freely giving the sinner grace, while only in the second stage of Condign merit was God placed in a debt. In other words the concept of grace is entirely swept away, but it is important to see that this is only as a result of Erasmus's views of free-will.

Luther accused Erasmus of contradicting himself. How could Erasmus speak of the will as being "ineffective" and in the same breath as able to accept or reject God's salvation because of an inherent power. "What," asks Luther, "is ineffective power but (in plain language) no power? So to say that 'free-will' exists and has power, albeit ineffective power, is . . . a contradiction in terms. It is like saying 'free-will' is something which is not free."

Luther asked Erasmus to explain precisely what he meant by the "inherent power of the sinner's will". How is it possible, and here Luther touched on a very profound issue and shows how much he was acquainted with the very Greek philosophers Erasmus knew so well—how is it possible for a *thing to move itself?* In other words, putting the issue in a wider context the question was this: How is it possible for the sinner's will (an abstract metaphysical concept, or, if you like, an abstract psychological concept) to be self-energising or self-propelling by its own internal energy? On the one hand this is a physiological and psychological impossibility, for then we would have to posit the same of the reason and the emotions, but more gravely this would mean that the will of the sinner could function autonomously and without reference to the darkness of his reason, the powerful bias towards sinful desires by the emotions, and without reference to his fallen nature! It would mean that the sinner's will functioned in a sort of isolation. And this is in fact asking us to believe far too much. The will must always be studied within the context of the entire fallen human nature, and never on its own.

Luther pointed out that if Erasmus insisted on a will that is free to choose God or reject Him, then of necessity it implied that the sinner's will has the inherent power to love God and His truth, for no one would choose God if he did not love Him. And once this is conceded, Erasmus is on the high road to Pelagianism which maintains that man can in fact love God and keep His law perfectly and so be the means of his own salvation. As Luther says: "If it can will and not will, it can also love and hate; and if it can love and hate, it can in measure keep the law and believe the gospel". Thus man can in fact will his own goodness and perfection! And naturally the converse is also true. If man can will his own goodness then, as Luther says: "What is here left to grace and the Holy Spirit? . . . What need of the Spirit or Christ, or God, if 'free-will' can overcome the motions of the mind to evil?"

As regards Erasmus's views that the use of free-will can actually lead to spiritual merit, Luther swept aside any verbal distinction between so-called Congruent merit and Condign merit. To him, any action performed independently of God which elicits a *reward* from God whether God rewards freely or under obligation, meant simply that salvation comes to man through God's response to what man has done! Thus

32

man saves himself in the last analysis. This Luther maintained vigorously, was an utter denial of the gospel of grace. Between "merit" and "grace" there can never be any compromise.

So far we have concentrated on Erasmus's views and Luther's exposure of them. We turn now to consider the positive side of Luther's teaching on man's will. Luther maintained that man is fallen in every part of his nature and personality.

When sin struck root in the nature of man it affected every part of him. It entered his reason and blinded it (II Cor. 4:4), it captured his emotions and man is now enslaved, in one way or another, to his lustful "drives" (Eph. 2:3) and it perverted his will and made it hostile to the things of God (John 3:20, Rom. 3:11, Matt. 23:37).

Worse still, the sinner is also part of Satan's kingdom, and indeed the Devil is said to hold him under his power (Eph. 2:2). As Luther said: ". . . he wants only to sin, and his choice is thus always sinful . . . The deepest truth about him is that his . . . power and exercise of choice, is *enslaved* to sin and Satan; and his natural condition is one of total inability to merit anything other than wrath and damnation".

To put it somewhat differently: man is a free agent in the sense that all his actions are genuinely spontaneous and arise from within himself, yet man is not at liberty to act in a way that is contrary to his fallen nature. If he were able then he could work out his own salvation; then he could reverse the thrust and bias of his nature; then he could dispel his own spiritual darkness, stop the sinful emotional drives, and free his will. True he acts freely, but always in harmony with his own sinful nature.

At this point Luther used Augustine's illustration of the two riders: "Man's will is like a beast standing between two riders. If God rides, it wills and goes where God wills . . . If Satan rides, it wills and goes where Satan wills. Nor may it choose to which rider it will run, or which it will seek; but the riders themselves fight to decide who shall have and hold it". If man could choose his own rider, his will would indeed be free, and he would be "sovereign" in his own "salvation".

To back up this assertion of his Luther gave some careful exegesis of a number of passages in Scripture, *i.e.* Rom. 1:18, 3:9f, 19f, 21-26, 8:5, John 1:5, 10-13, 16, John 6.

Luther regarded man's fall with intense seriousness and drew the line right through, no matter how hard or difficult it might seem to him. Let sin be sin, in order that grace might be grace, this was his solemn belief. ·

(c) *Does the loss of free-will make the sinner a victim of compulsion?*

Erasmus seemed to imply that Luther believed that because man's will was fallen, and because God's will would ultimately triumph in history, therefore men were under the necessity of compulsion. They were more or less machines through whom God exercised His Sovereignty.

Luther strongly denied this. When he spoke of necessity he spoke, not of a necessity of compulsion, but of a necessity of immutability. There is a subtle but very vital distinction here. Let Luther explain: "A man without the Spirit of God does not do evil against his will, under pressure, as though he were taken by the scruff of the neck and dragged into it, like a thief or footpad being dragged off against his will to punishment; but he does it spontaneously and voluntarily. He goes on willingly and desiring to do evil. This is what we mean by necessity of immutability; that the will cannot change itself, nor give itself another bent". The will of the sinner is so fixed in sin and enslaved—not by outward compulsion —but simply because it has an inward and constant attachment to evil, that we can say that it is immutably fixed in its sinful path. It is the immutability of a never-ending stream of dirty water that springs constantly from the heart of a polluted fountain. It is not compelled to be dirty, but its very nature gives it such an inevitability.

(d) *The commands of Scripture imply ability.*

Erasmus's argument was straightforward here: it is ridiculous to exhort men to have faith and repent, if they did not possess the ability to do so. In reply Luther showed that the commands of Scripture were given, not to indicate or imply that man has the ability to comply with them, but rather to show man his utter weakness in *not* being able to comply with them. The law was given, not to indicate that we might keep it and so be justified by the law, but to be a schoolmaster to bring us to Christ, to show us God's standard and demands, to crush us beneath its weight of condemnation and judgment.

If Erasmus's proposition were true, then he would be proving more than he actually had proposed to prove: that grace is unnecessary. If the commands of Scripture proved man's ability to fulfil them, then obviously he can fulfil them; and, if he can fulfil them, he does not need God's grace! So, for example, if Christ's command to love the Lord our God with all our heart and soul and mind implied that we could do that, then we do not need God's regenerating grace to enable us to do it.

We must remember that we are here once more in the realm of mystery. How can we, as preachers of the Gospel, plead with men to repent and believe in the Lord Jesus Christ, when we know very well that they are so sunk in sin that they *cannot* do it? It makes no sense to human reason. The greatness of Luther lay in the fact that he insisted that we should hold truth in balance without seeking to rationalise it. Certain it is that man in his sin loves darkness and is so fallen that he has no free-will to repent and believe. Yet, it is just as certain that we are to present the Gospel and call on men to believe! Luther maintained that we must both accept the sinner's true condition and also press him to accept Christ. The solution of this antinomy is to be found finally in God alone, and what we must avoid is man-made bridges that seek to rationalise these two truths into a position where they seem more reasonable.

Conclusion

You will have realised that Luther's concept of free-will, or rather "the bondage of the will" raises questions of great moment and gravity. Some of these we now consider.

(1) *Was Luther Biblical?*

Is the Reformed doctrine Scriptural? As far as Luther himself goes, all we can say is: Read his work and you will see how thoroughly he attempts to base his view upon Scripture as he seeks to expound passage after passage as faithfully as possible. Luther's view arose from within Scripture; he certainly did not impose it upon Scripture wilfully and deliberately. By contrast, Erasmus's attempts at exegesis are insignificant. The Scripture *is after all* our only guide, and the question is this: How do the exponents of free-will explain the spiritual death that Adam and Eve died consequent to their disobedience? Did that involve the fall of the *whole* nature of man or not? How is it possible for man's reason to be blinded and his emotions held captive in sinful drives and lusts, and yet for his will to have retained a kind of neutrality, no, more, an inherent power to choose God if it decides to do so? What do they make of Eph. 2:1-4 with its analysis of the sinner before regeneration, "dead in trespasses and sins" and needing to be quickened by the Spirit? How do they explain the vicious malignity poured out upon Christ in the days of His flesh? Surely if men's wills were neutral, or could respond to a little prompting by God this would have been the occasion during which to exercise their free-wills. And yet there is this violent reaction against Him and in the end His disciples also desert Him!

If men are at enmity with God why should they suddenly decide to accept Him? And if we say that God "helps" them, or "leads" them, or "enables" them, what do we mean by those terms? Surely it is not just the will which needs to be helped, but the entire nature of the man which needs regeneration before his reason can see the Truth, before his emotions can enter into a new direction, before he can exercise his will to accept Christ! Man is either a total slave or not.

(2) *If we do accept free-will can we explain that final, fateful decision of the sinner to trust Christ other than in terms of chance?*

If the great issue lies finally in the hand of the sinner, and Christ has to stand outside the door and knock, waiting for the sinner to open, then *what is it* that finally makes one sinner decide and another not? Is it more information? The sinner's temperament? The appealing nature of the preacher? The atmosphere? Because he has had a less bitter experience of life? Spurgeon asks the same question in the "Sword and Trowel" of 1887: "But what caused you thus to turn? What sacred force was that which turned you from sin to righteousness? Do you attribute this singular renewal to the existence of a something better in you than has been yet discovered in your unconverted neighbour?"

What then is it that propels an unregenerate will to turn from sin to Christ? The sinner himself, deciding against the entire bias of his nature? This is incredible to say the least!

(3) *How does this affect our preaching and evangelism?*

Does it negate evangelistic effort? On the contrary, from a study of Church history the very opposite seems to be the case. We have already mentioned that the vast majority of Reformers believed that man's will was so enslaved in sin that only God could loosen it. But this was also the case with some of the choicest evangelists in the Church's history: George Whitefield, C. H. Spurgeon, Brownlow North, Jonathan Edwards, William Carey and some of the Welsh revivalists. Indeed it is rather revealing to study the hymns of Charles Wesley (who together with his brother John opposed some of Whitefield's Calvinistic views). In a well known hymn he writes:

"Long my imprisoned spirit lay
Fast bound in sin and nature's night:
Thine eye diffused a quickening ray;
I woke; the dungeon flamed with light;
My chains fell off: my heart was free:
I rose, went forth and followed Thee."

This prompted old "Rabbi" Duncan to ask: "Where's your Arminianism now, friend?"

The point was that both Luther, his fellow Reformers and the so-called "Reformed" or "Calvinistic" evangelists never tried to rationalise on this issue beyond a certain point. To them it was enough that the sinner was "fast bound in sin and nature's night", chained in a dungeon; at the same time it was also enough that God had ordained preaching as the means of evangelism. So, too, God has revealed to us that it is our solemn responsibility to present Christ to the sinner, to plead with him to repent, and to exhort him to believe in Jesus Christ. This we must do because God has ordained it. True, we believe that God's elect will respond, and that God will draw them in, but Luther insisted on the fact that we are simply to do what God has ordained and leave it at that.

36

In other words we are faced here with a kind of antinomy. Iain Murray puts it very well, when writing about Spurgeon he says: "He unceasingly set forth the greatness of Christ's love to sinners, the freeness of His pardon and the fulness of His atonement; and he persuaded and exhorted all to repent and trust in such a Saviour. The point at which he diverged from both hyper-Calvinism and Arminianism is that he refused to rationalise *how* men can be commanded to do what is not in their power. Arminians say that sinners are commanded, therefore, they must be able; hyper-Calvinists say they are not able, therefore they cannot be commanded. But Scripture and Calvinism sets forth *both* man's inability and his duty, and both truths are a necessary part of evangelism—the former reveals the sinner's need of a help which only God can give, and the latter . . . shows him the place in which his peace and safety lies, namely the Person of the Son of God.

"Spurgeon too held these two truths, man's duty to believe and his sinful inability to do so, and used them like the two jaws of a vice to grip the sinner's conscience."

And is this not precisely what we do when we preach the Law? Man must keep the Law of God to be righteous before God, but he cannot! Thus the sinner is thrown into what is sometimes called "evangelical" despair. Caught between truths, he is forced to turn ultimately to God and cry to God for mercy; he is forced to look to Christ who has kept the Law perfectly. Similarly, we must portray man as utterly fallen, with his reason, emotion and will in the dungeon, and at the same time we must exhort him to repent and have faith in Christ, for this is his only salvation! And if the sinner cries out in despair: "But I cannot, I am too ensnared, too loaded down with chains; I cannot even believe," then at that moment in despair he comes to an end of himself in every sense of the word. What is left? Nothing, except that he now throws his arms out to Christ and pleads with Him: "I cannot save myself, I cannot keep the Law, I do not love Thee, I cannot even repent for my heart is too sinful and hard, I cannot even believe, oh! Help me, Save me!" And to the question whether God will respond to such a sinner's cry, we gladly and unhesitatingly reply: Of course! Has He not clearly said: 'Whoever shall call on the Lord's Name shall be saved".

From man's vantage point it is precisely at this moment, at the sinner's last gasp, that God intervenes and quickens the will of the sinner. From God's viewpoint, he has been working *already* in the sinner's heart bringing him low so that He can save him completely.

This evangelism is surely close to the New Testament though it is in direct contrast to that which we have today where the sinner virtually casts a vote and "decides" to turn to God and accept Christ out of his own strength.

It must surely also be clear that the biblical and Reformed position is as far removed from hyper-Calvinism as it is from Arminianism. If Arminianism is dangerous, hyper-Calvinism is even more so. The hyper-Calvinist falls into the error of extreme logic and rationalism, feeling that if the sinner is elect, everything should be left to God. The Reformed position is that man is unable of his own free-will to turn to God, but also in obedience to God every man must be called to repentance and faith. If someone says that that doesn't make sense, it is admitted that humanly speaking it seems to be contradictory. This position is maintained first of all because God has commanded it. He has revealed His truth and we are to receive it. We do not throw out other major Christian doctrines (such as Inspiration, the Atonement or the Incarnation) because there are aspects of them which appear to be contrary to human logic. We should not in this case either. Secondly, this position is maintained because we do not know how and where God is working. We cannot see into the sinner's heart and mind to know whether God is already at work calling and quickening him. What we can do is present Christ in the power of the Spirit and fulfil our solemn obligation of pleading with Him with all our might—beyond which no gimmicks, emotional pressure, "easy steps" or anything else will raise a dead man to life. Only God Himself can do that.

Thus while the denial of free-will seems to defy human reason it only underlies the fact that God works in and through our very helplessness; helplessness to understand it all fully, the helplessness of the preacher in his own strength, the helplessness of a slick campaign devoid of the Spirit, and the helplessness of the sinner to lift even the smallest finger towards his redemption, indeed his helplessness even to repent and believe without God's energising power.

What is grace? The answer is found in Isa. 65: ". . . I am found of them that sought me not; I said, Behold me, behold me, unto a nation that was not called by my name".

Apart from Luther himself there is the striking testimony to God's powerful grace in the life of Pastor Hsi. A Confucianist scholar, utterly addicted to opium, helplessly chained by sin, darkness and hostility to the Gospel, unwilling to even listen to C.I.M. missionaries led by David Hill, he was clearly brought into an experience of God's grace by the sovereign power of God. Step by step, in a series of extraordinary providences, all his efforts to evade the missionaries and their message were frustrated by God. At last he not only found himself a most unwilling guest in the mission compound, but also arrested by the Gospel story as he read it in the Bible. One day, all alone while reading the Bible, he was finally overwhelmed by God's grace and became a believer in Christ, happy to sit "in willing bonds beneath His feet!" The same was the Apostle Paul's experience. Full of hatred and malignity, breathing out vengeance and murder, utterly hostile to the Gospel, God laid him low with one stroke of grace!

And, although we do not always know it in such a dramatic manner, this is the experience of every Christian. The mercy of God's grace is that it does for us what we are incapable of doing for ourselves, it breathes life into the dead spiritual nature, transforms the mind, will and emotions and so enables sinners to respond freely when God draws them to Himself. His grace makes sinners willing in the day of His power.

May God give us the grace to be very wise and balanced in handling this great truth; may we be true to Scripture, honest with the sinner, faithful and fervent in our preaching, and above all, faithful to God who has made us co-workers with Himself in the Gospel of Grace.

GOD'S CHURCH
and
SCRIPTURAL
EVANGELISM

David Kingdon

IN THE EVANGELICAL WORLD AT THE PRESENT TIME THERE IS A WIDESPREAD rethinking of the subject of evangelism. Indeed, it would not be an exaggeration to say that evangelism, as traditionally understood, is in the melting-pot.

Various factors have combined to bring about this situation. In the first place, there is increasing disappointment with the results of mass evangelistic campaigns. The paucity of lasting results has contrasted with

41

their soaring costs. The claims of some evangelists that their campaigns indicated the beginning of revival have proved unfounded. Many evangelicals are now beginning to ask whether the time has not come for a critical scrutiny of mass evangelism in the light of Scripture.

In the second place, the increasing tendency towards what can be termed "ecumenical evangelism" has raised the question in some minds as to the biblical justification for co-operating with all shades of theological opinion in united evangelism. Those evangelical churches which are opposed to the Ecumenical movement on what they believe to be biblical grounds are coming to see that it is thoroughly inconsistent to become involved in ecumenical evangelism. If one unites with modernists one week in evangelism how can one refuse to discuss church unity with them the next? Certainly one cannot with any consistency do the former and refuse to do the latter.

Thirdly, the way in which entertainment has invaded evangelism is causing serious-minded Christians increasing concern. When they read the New Testament they are struck by the contrast between Paul's refusal to preach with enticing words of man's wisdom and the blatant parading of personalities and the encouragement of personal followings which is so marked a feature of modern evangelism.

Fourthly, in the United Kingdom—and one sees evidence of it beginning to happen elsewhere—there has been a rediscovery of Puritan theology and, with it, a re-awakening of interest in a kind of evangelism which stands in stark contrast with the evangelism of the past few generations. It has come to be appreciated that men like Joseph Alleine, John Bunyan, Jonathan Edwards, George Whitefield, the two Wesleys, Murray McCheyne and C. H. Spurgeon were powerful preachers of the Gospel whose presuppositions, message and methods were markedly different from those which are in vogue today.

For these reasons, then, there is a widespread questioning of tradition and a willingness to examine time-worn practices in the light of Scripture.

I

Biblical evangelism is rooted in the biblical doctrine of God because it is here that evangelism finds its source and motive power. But exactly how, you may ask, does the biblical doctrine of God bear upon the subject of evangelism? Here are just three vital aspects:—

(i) God is creator and judge

"In the beginning God created the heaven and the earth" (Gen. 1:1). The world and all that is within it owes its existence to the God who spoke

His creative words and brought the universe into being. All men owe to God as Creator the homage and loyalty of their hearts. All men are called upon to acknowledge their dependence and to express their thanksgiving in praise and devotion to the living God.

Moreover since God is "the judge of all the earth" they are accountable to Him for what they are and what they do. In His righteous judgment He will "render to every man according to his deeds" (Rom. 2:6). Since He is omnipresent no one can hide from Him (Psa. 139), and so His judgments are always based upon a perfect knowledge of the accused.

It is only as the character of God as creator and judge is held forth in preaching that the enormity of man's sinful rebellion and the folly of his impiety are exposed. This the apostle Paul does in Romans 1, for example. Man in sin refuses to glorify God his Creator (v. 21) and thankfully to acknowledge his dependence upon God for every good gift. Rather he turns to creation and lavishes love upon the creature which is due only to God. To plead ignorance will not do since the clear revelation in the created order of the eternal power and deity of God leaves him absolutely without excuse (v. 20). Man in sin is thus condemned before ever he hears the Gospel. He is condemned because he has "changed the truth of God into a lie, and worshipped and served the creature rather than the *Creator*, who is blessed for ever" (v. 25).

Therefore, only as the doctrine of God the creator and judge is expounded can the wickedness of man's apostate heart be brought home to him. Our evangelism must not begin with man's *need* but with his *sin,* and his sin can only be seen for what it is—rebellion, impiety and ingratitude—as the doctrine of the sovereign creator and eternal judge is brought to his attention.

(ii) God is holy and righteous
The holiness and righteousness of God cannot be left out of evangelistic preaching since the result will be an impoverished view of salvation. The grace of God in salvation can only be appreciated and captivate the heart of the sinner if he first is made aware of the holiness of God, for slight views of God inevitably issue in slight views of sin, and slight views of sin issue in slight views of Christ's death on the Cross.

The holiness of God finds expression in His majesty and in His awful purity. In His majesty He is "high and lifted up" (Isa. 6:1), enthroned above the earth, reigning in utter sovereignty. This God of majesty cannot be manipulated by man; He is not at man's beck and call. He is sovereign majesty, and thus He saves whom He will (Rom. 9:15-16). God is not the subject of man; rather man is subject to the sovereign will of God. The God of the Bible is not forced to save any man. Only in the sovereignty of grace is the sinner chosen, called, regenerated, justified, adopted, sanctified and glorified.

God's holiness is not only manifested in the separateness of His majesty, but also in the absolute moral purity of His Being. "He is light, and in Him is no darkness at all." He dwells in unapproachable light, and reacts with indescribable wrath against sin. To realise this is to be brought face to face with one's own defilement, against which the door of heaven will remain for ever shut (Rev. 21:27).

The righteousness of God is closely related to His holiness, but there is a significant difference of meaning which it is important to notice. The basic idea conveyed by the Hebrew word *tsedeq* is that of conformity to a norm. Thus "righteous balances" are balances which conform to the norm, whereas "unrighteous" balances are such because they deviate from the norm. Therefore, to say that God is righteous is to say that God is the norm for all conduct. Now the righteousness of God is the measure by which man is judged. "He shall judge the world with righteousness" (Psa. 96:13; cf. 98:9) is the witness of the Old Testament, which is taken up and reiterated in the New Testament proclamation. Thus Paul assured the scoffing Athenians that God "hath appointed a day, in the which he will judge the world in righteousness by that man whom he hath ordained; whereof he hath given assurance in that he hath raised him from the dead" (Acts 17:31).

God in judgment will never act unrighteously, nor can He act unrighteously to save sinners. He saves sinners not in spite of His righteousness, as some preachers suggest when they oppose His mercy to His righteousness, but because He *is* righteous. In the Gospel, mercy is not warring against righteousness precisely because in the Gospel "is the righteousness of God revealed from faith to faith" (Rom. 1:17).

Unless the righteousness of God is proclaimed in the kerygma, neither the sinner's terrible deviation from the norm, God Himself, nor the necessity of propitiation can be appreciated. Whilst many evangelicals uphold substitutionary atonement, few seem to appreciate the importance of the atonement as *propitiation*—the rendering of a righteous God propitious towards the sinner because His righteousness is upheld and His wrath assuaged. Not that we should view the atonement as constraining the love of God toward elect sinners, because the atonement is itself constrained by the love of God. "Herein is love, not that we loved God but that He loved us, and sent His Son to be the propitiation for our sins" (I John 4:10). Nonetheless, the atoning death of Christ at once reconciled the Father to the elect and provided the ground on which they can be reconciled to Him (II Cor. 5:19).

(iii) The character of God is expressed in His law
The holiness and righteousness of God are not left undefined and vague in Scripture. Rather they focus in, and are expressed by, His Law. Sin is in consequence particularised as "the transgression of the law" (I John

3:4; cf. Rom. 4:15). Though sin has psychological consequences, for example a sense of anxiety and disharmony, it is not defined in Scripture so much in psychological terms as in terms of transgression against the revealed commandments of the God who demands, "Be ye holy, for I am holy" (I Pet. 1:16). Sin therefore has an objective character as transgression resulting from disobedience (Eph. 2:2). And transgression renders the sinner guilty before God.

This emphasis of Scripture upon the moral law runs clean counter to much contemporary evangelicalism. Today the Gospel is often given a psychological orientation—it is presented in terms of man's need for freedom from anxiety and from inward disharmony. Now while the Gospel of Christ has within it the power to make man whole, the subjective benefits of reconciliation (so far as man's *experience* of them is concerned) must not be allowed to obscure the fact that man is a transgressor before God. His transgression of God's law must be brought home to him, and this can only be brought about as the law is preached and applied in the power of the Holy Spirit. To preach the Gospel in terms of man's *psychological* needs is in fact to preach a man-centred Gospel. God's redemptive purposes are limited by, and made subordinate to, the needs of man as he sees them.

The preaching of the character of God as expressed in His law-demands serves to emphasise to the sinner the perfections of God ("the law is holy, and the commandment holy, and just, and good . . . the law is spiritual"—Rom. 7:12, 14) and the hatred of, and unbelief in, God which are resident in his apostate heart. Since the commandments were not given that man might win the love of God, but as the means whereby he might prove his love to God (cf. Exod. 20:6, "that *love* me and keep my commandments"; I John 5:3; John 14:15), man's transgression of the commandments demonstrates his enmity against God. Thus, the preaching of the law is indispensable in the creation of a conviction of the exceeding sinfulness of sin.

Furthermore, without the preaching of the law human inability will not be appreciated. The law-demands of God demonstrate the inability of the sinner to please God, and thus point to the necessity of the satisfaction of Christ as redeemer. "For what the law could not do in that it was weak through the flesh, God sending His own Son in the likeness of sinful flesh, and for sin, condemned sin in the flesh" (Rom. 8:3).

Any evangelism which does not set forth the law will inevitably produce slight views of the redeeming work of Christ. To be told, for example, that to give our lives to Christ is the noblest thing we can do, is failing to appreciate that, as sinners, we can do nothing noble—we cannot please God. On the other hand, when our heart's corruption and our utter inability are brought home to us by the preaching of the law we cry "God be merciful to me, *the* sinner" (Luke 18:13).

James Denney insisted that every evangelist must be a theologian. If this is so, what is most urgently needed today is a recovery of the biblical doctrine of God, without which the Gospel of grace is cheapened.

II

If the biblical doctrine of God is essential to biblical evangelism, no less is the biblical doctrine of man in sin.

Three views of man in his present condition suggest discussion. It is possible to maintain that man is *healthy*. This is in essence the view of humanism in its various forms. That man is healthy is the basic premise of most modern educational theory and of political philosophies, such as Communism, which believe in the perfectibility of man. What problems man faces are not due to himself but to his environment. In this view of man, therefore, all talk of sin, guilt, pollution and inability are out of place since *within himself* man has the resources to solve all his problems.

Secondly, it can be argued that man is *sick*. To get better he needs, therefore, to go to a doctor and, after his diagnosis, faithfully to take the prescribed medicine. This view of man may be described as the semi-Pelagian. It is characteristic of both Roman Catholic theology and much contemporary evangelicalism. In the Roman Catholic form of Pelagianism man is pictured as needing the help of sacramental grace; in the Protestant, as needing the help of the Holy Spirit. In either case "grace" is seen in terms of God's *help* towards recovery.

The third view of man is, I believe, that which is taught in Scripture. According to this, man is neither healthy nor sick; he is "*dead* in trespasses and sins" (Eph. 2:1). In this condition, he is not free for he walks "according to the course of this world, according to the prince of the power of the air, the spirit that now worketh in the children of disobedience" (v. 2). His will is enslaved, his mind is darkened, his affections are misdirected. He cannot please God.

A dead man needs more than medicine—he needs resurrection. Thus, Paul consistently speaks of the work of God in elect sinners in the following ways: making alive together with Christ (Eph. 2:5; Col. 2:13 *sunzōopoeio*); begetting, *gennaō*—that is, implanting life (John 1:13; 3:3-8; I Pet. 1:23; I John 2:29), and creating (Eph. 2:10; 4:24, ktizo).

The biblical view of man has certain important implications for evangelism. In the first place, it casts the preacher of the Gospel in total dependence upon the work of the Holy Spirit. Unless he works with and by the Word there can be no conversions. Thus the preacher is shut up to prayer, that the anointing of the Spirit may rest upon the proclamation of the Gospel. Since he cannot create one anxious thought, he must rely entirely upon the Holy Spirit to convict of sin, righteousness and judgment (John 16:8-11).

Secondly, preaching can never be an end in itself; it must be a means to an end—the conversion of sinners. The end of Paul's preaching was never to attract attention to himself, but it was the means used by God to draw sinners to the crucified Christ. "My speech and my preaching were not with enticing words of man's wisdom, but in demonstration of the Spirit and of power." Paul could say this, because it was his determined aim "not to know anything among you, save Jesus Christ, and Him crucified" (I Cor. 2:2, 4). It is impossible to square Paul's attitude with the personality cults and publicity organisations of mass evangelism.

Thirdly, once a preacher is persuaded of the biblical view of man certain consequences will follow both for his presentation of the Gospel and the application of it to his hearers.

The presentation of the Gospel will be governed by the biblical doctrine of God. It will be instilled with a sense of reverence and awesome wonder that such a God so loved that He gave His only begotten Son. In *His* name the preacher holds forth the Word of life to perishing sinners. Having also the scriptural view of the plight of man the preacher will show that "only Jesus can do *helpless* sinners good". In short, he will preach as a dying man to dying men, with solemnity and earnestness.

As to method, on the one hand the preacher must apply the Gospel to his hearers and, on the other, he will foreswear all devices and stratagems which would suggest that men can save themselves. Realising that the heart of man is "deceitful above all things and desperately wicked", he will seek to root the sinner out of all the refuges into which he creeps to hide from the living God and His Word. The Gospel must be applied to sinners in a particular and detailed way or the citadel of man's soul will not be taken. As is hand to hand fighting by the infantry to an artillery bombardment, so is the detailed application of the Gospel related to its general exposition. A city is not taken until the enemy is flushed out of its cellars.

On the other hand, all methods which leave the sinner with the impression that he can save himself will be foresworn. When some young people who had already "been out to the front" asked, when present when another appeal was made, "Pastor do we have to go out again? We have *done* it once", is there not something radically wrong with the whole appeal system? Does it not suggest that the appeal must be responded to in order to be saved? Is there not a disastrous confusion between going forward and going to Christ by faith alone? The fact that Leighton Ford argues the case for the appeal system largely on psychological grounds should give us food for thought, for this suggests that it is man's psychological make-up which in the last analysis is to determine how the Gospel is to be applied to him.

Some reading this may be prepared to defend the appeal system on the pragmatic ground that it works. Aside from the fact that the Church did nicely without the system for eighteen-and-a-half centuries, there is the incipient and ubiquitous danger of pragmatism. That danger is this—that the *more* something works the better. Thus William Sargant in "Battle for the Mind", after expounding Pavlov's theory of conditioned reflexes, and comparing the Communist brain-washing techniques which are built thereon with *certain* evangelistic techniques, argues that the Church would make more converts if she used the same methods! The moral is too obvious to need pointing.

Some may be prepared to argue that it is possible to draw a distinction between the message and the methods. However, methods express presuppositions; there is no such thing as a *neutral* method, for every method in evangelism expresses both a certain view of God and a certain view of man. However time-worn methods are they must all be thoroughly subjected to the scrutiny of Scripture, to discover whether they are glorifying to God and in the best interests of man.

III

How about the function of the Church in evangelism? It is here that we are most obviously weak as evangelicals. There is a reason for this. When, in the 19th century, hitherto evangelical denominations largely departed from the truth of the Gospel, those evangelicals who remained within began to develop extra-church organisations, in which they could co-operate in evangelism with like-minded believers in other communions. The co-operation was not on a Church basis, but on an individual or group basis. The result has been that evangelicals have got on with evangelism, whilst leaving others to concentrate on the doctrine of the church.

When one compares present-day evangelism with the evangelism described in the New Testament, certain differences emerge quite sharply.

For a start, the evangelism of the New Testament was *church* evangelism. It was church based and the whole Church was involved.

Evangelism, as described in the Acts of the Apostles and in the Epistles, is through the Church to the world. Never does evangelism find expression in extra-church organisations. The local Church is God's unit, indeed God's organism, for the evangelisation of a district or region. Thus from the Church of the Thessalonians the Word of the Lord sounded out to Macedonia and Achaia (I Thess. 1:8). It is into the local Church, the body of Christ in its local manifestation, that new converts were brought by baptism. It is in the local Church that they found nurture,

48

received instruction and came under discipline. Evangelism was not the work of the enthusiastic few but of the mobilised many. We get a glimpse of this communal evangelism in Acts 8:4, where we are told that after the persecution consequent upon the death of Stephen believers were scattered from Jerusalem and they "went every where preaching the Word".

The reason for all this is not hard to find. According to the teaching of the New Testament the purposes of God centre in the *Church*—its calling by grace, its worship, mission, edification, sanctification and justification. For the *Church* Christ gave Himself "that He might sanctify and cleanse it with the washing of water by the word, that He might present it to Himself a glorious church, not having spot, or wrinkle, or any such thing, but that it should be holy and without blemish" (Eph. 5:26-27). Thus we who make much of the evangel, which proclaims the glorious redemption wrought in Christ, fail to be faithful to the whole counsel of God if we do not realise that Gospel and Church belong inseparably together.

Because God's purposes centre in the Church, it is not possible to take an individualistic view of salvation which would allow a slight view of the Church to be taken. Implicit in the idea of our faith-union with Christ, is the thought that in Him we are a new humanity. There are but two basic solidarities in human existence; the solidarity of mankind in Adam, and the solidarity of regenerate believers in Christ, the last Adam, who is the quickener of the dead. "As in Adam all die, even so in Christ shall all be made alive" (I Cor. 15:22). If Adam is the federal head of the old humanity, so Christ is the head of the new humanity. As in virtue of their union with Adam, his sin was imputed to all men (Rom. 5:12-14) so in virtue of our union with Christ by faith, His righteousness is imputed to us (Rom. 5:18-19). While it is true that we are *individually* granted faith to believe in Christ, and thus are justified, it is also true that our union with Christ does not permit us to take an *individualistic* view of salvation. We are not saved to be isolated units, we are saved in Christ, and thus are incorporated into a new humanity, *one* new man (Eph. 2:15).

Undoubtedly, one of the great weaknesses of contemporary evangelism lies in the failure of so many evangelicals to appreciate that conversion is not an end in itself, but the means whereby the believer is incorporated into the new humanity which is in Christ. So much present-day evangelism seems to proceed on the assumption that a complete silence about the Church—its purpose, nature, and destiny—is the mark of faithfulness to the Gospel proclaimed by the Apostles.

Until we recover the apostles' doctrine of the Church we shall not recover the apostles' practice of evangelism. However, apostolic evangelism was not building-centred. A study of Paul's "methods", if such be the right word, demonstrates this. Often he preaches in the open air, in the market-place and by the riverside at Philippi, on Mars Hill at Athens.

He got into synagogues where he could and preached Sabbath by Sabbath as long as he was allowed to do so. At Corinth he even opened up next door to the synagogue after his message was rejected in it.

Paul's evangelism, then, though it was church-centred, was not building-centred, as so much of our evangelism is. Indeed it is true to say that very little evangelism was carried on when the church met together. The church met together for worship and instruction rather than for an evangelistic service. The very incidental nature of the reference to the coming of an unbeliever into a service of worship demonstrates this (I Cor. 14:24 ff.).

Going into all the world is hardly carried out by preaching the Gospel at a stated time on Sunday evenings. Evangelism must be through the whole church to the whole world The trouble is that as someone has said, too many people are singing "Standing on the Promises" while sitting on the premises!

Lastly, we must say a few words about the church's task of maintaining an uncompromised testimony in evangelism. Paul did not hold joint evangelistic services with the Synagogue, precisely because he believed that to the church had been committed the truth. The tendency today is to be pragmatic—to join with anyone who is prepared to co-operate in evangelism regardless of whether he preaches the Gospel or not. The apostle who wrote the epistle to the Galatians would never have done so. With anyone who preached works as being the ground of our salvation Paul would not co-operate. Rather he said, "let him be accursed" (Gal. 1:9). Yet it is now fashionable for some evangelicals to co-operate with sacramentalists on the one hand and outright modernists on the other. It has been forgotten that the Scriptures do say that the church is "the pillar and ground of truth" (I Tim. 3:15).

If we co-operate with everybody, we sow confusion as to the nature of the Gospel and the exclusiveness of salvation as it is in Christ Jesus. Furthermore, we put ourselves under the obligation of forwarding proposed converts to churches which deny the very Gospel we preach. You would hardly expect a Marxist to send one of his converts to the Monday Club.[1]

Of course, where churches in a particular area are in substantial agreement there may well be co-operation. What I am so opposed to is quite different—evangelism which is not based upon such biblical authority.

In conclusion, we must face some hard facts. We have failed to evangelise as we should. We have been guilty of silence, apathy and lack of compassion. We must repent before God, and open our hearts afresh to His love for lost sinners, and with burning zeal go into all the world preaching Christ crucified, risen and exalted, the only hope of sinners.

[1] A club in England patronised by devout right-wing Conservatives.

SECULARISM and the GOSPEL

David Kingdon

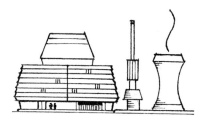

IT IS EXTREMELY IMPORTANT THAT WE BE CLEAR AS TO WHAT WE UNDER-
stand by the terms "secular", "secularisation" and "secularism". I
propose, therefore, to begin by examining these and then to attempt to
frame a workable definition of the term "secular". It is necessary to do
this in order to have a proper frame of reference.

51

1. Secularism and Secularisation

The English word "secular" derives from the Latin word "saeculum" meaning "this age". There is also another term denoting "world" and that is "mundus". "Saeculum" is a time-word, used frequently to translate the Greek word "eon", which means "age" or "epoch". "Mundus", on the other hand, is a space-word, used most frequently to translate the Greek word "cosmos" which means "the universe" or "the created order". Now this ambiguity goes back to a basic difference between Greek and Hebrew views of reality. In essence the difference amounts to this: that the Greeks conceived of reality spatially, the Hebrews temporally.

Harvey Cox, in his well known book, *The Secular City*, puts the difference in the following way:

"For the Greeks, the world was a place, a location. Happenings of interest could occur within the world, but nothing significant ever happened *to* the world. There is no such thing as world history. For the Hebrews, on the other hand, the world was *essentially* history, a series of events beginning with Creation and heading toward a Consummation. Thus the Greeks perceived existence spatially; the Hebrews perceived it temporally. The tension between the two has plagued Christian theology since its outset" (p. 18).

Now if Cox is right, and I believe that he is (at this point), then we have to ask ourselves how far the traditional distinction between the secular and the sacred rests upon an unbiblical dualism. Certainly in Christian history it has done so. It has carried the notion of inferiority. Thus a "secular" priest was (and still is in Roman Catholicism) regarded as inferior in status to the cloistered religions, for the one was in the world and the other was out of it. It seems to me that the same type of unbiblical dualism is often reflected in the way in which the distinction between "this worldly" and "other worldly" is drawn in evangelicalism. I remember Christian students at Cambridge talking of their academic work and their Christian service in antithetical terms: "my academic work" and "my work for Christ", as if the former were somehow outside of the design of God for them.

Several recent writers have drawn a sharp distinction between "secularism" and "secularisation". Those who draw this distinction tend to view "secularism" as a bad, and "secularisation" as a good thing. Harvey Cox says, "Secularism . . . is the name for an ideology, a new closed world view which functions much like a new religion" (p. 21). Charles Davis in his Maurice lectures (1966) published under the title *God's Grace in History* offers this definition: "Secularism as commonly understood is agnostic humanism. Empiricism usually underlies it. Secularists are by conviction anti-metaphysical and generally exclude any knowledge of

52

what lies outside the range of empirical verification. This is irreconcilable with Christian faith" (p. 11).

Secularisation, on the other hand, is seen by writers like Cox, Davis (with some reservations), Van Buren and Colin Williams as basically a good thing and as indeed the outworking of the Gospel in world history. C. A. van Peursen defines secularisation as the deliverance of man "first from religions and then from metaphysical control over his reason and his language" (quoted by Cox, p. 2). Cox sees the process of secularisation as resulting from the biblical faith. The biblical doctrine of creation results in the *disenchantment of nature*, for the Bible separates nature from God and distinguishes man from nature, thus ruling out animism and all forms of magic.

"This disenchantment of the natural world provides," says Cox, "an absolute precondition for the development of natural science" (p. 24). In this remark he is undoubtedly correct, for unless man can observe the natural world unafraid, no true science is possible. The development of modern science has taken place within the Judaeo-Christian tradition because the biblical doctrine of creation alone makes science possible. Nature is uniform, it is subject to law, because of God's creative work and His sustaining activity. Without this induction would be impossible. We may certainly agree with Cox and others that secularisation, in this aspect, is the outworking of the biblical faith. But we shall not, as biblical Christians, be able to draw the conclusion that Bonhoeffer does, in the often quoted passage from his *Letters and Papers from Prison*. He argues that man has now "come of age", that he is called to live as if God did not exist, because the process of secularisation has pushed God out of life. "God is teaching us that we must live as men who can get along very well without Him. The God who is with us is the God who forsakes us (Mark 15:34). The God who makes us live in this world without using Him as a working hypothesis is the God before whom we are ever standing. Before God and with Him we live without God?" (*Letters and Papers*, p. 122).

Apart from any criticisms which may be brought against Bonhoeffer's verbal juggling (see E. L. Mascall: *The Secularisation of Christianity*, pp. 41-42), the most serious charge which may be brought against Bonhoeffer, and those who accept his conclusions, is that what he sees as proof of man's maturity is in fact the proof of his apostasy. Man as sinner is able to live in a world ordered and governed by God as though God did not exist. He accepts as the premise for his scientific activity the orderliness of the cosmos, but refuses to acknowledge his Creator. He engages in experimentation without recognising that he only does so because he is God's image-bearer. Secular man is thus as guilty as pre-secular man. Like him he lives in God's world which declares His eternal power and deity, and like him he worships and serves the creature more than the Creator (Rom. 1:20, 25).

Cox sees as another characteristic of secularisation what he calls the *desacralisation of politics*. In a sacral society political power has a religious legitimation. Thus in the Roman Empire the Emperor was both political ruler and "pontifex maximus". Cox argues that the Exodus is a pivotal event in the desacralisation of politics. "It was," he says, "an act of insurrection against a duly constituted monarch, a pharaoh whose relationship to the sun-god reconstituted his claim to political sovereignty. It become the central event around which the Hebrews organised their whole perception of reality." He then draws this astounding conclusion. "As such, it symbolised the deliverance of man out of a sacral-political order and into history and social change, out of religiously legitimated monarchs and into a world where political leadership would be based on power gained by the capacity to accomplish specific social objectives" (p. 28).

To make such a statement Cox must overlook the fact that Israel from the Exodus onwards was a sacral society, under Moses, the Judges and the Kings. Moreover, it is very much an open question whether Greek ideas such as the concept of democracy and the Romantic assumption of a social contract have not been more responsible for the desacralisation of politics than the biblical faith. Charles Davis, rightly to my mind, sounds a note of caution. He suggests that the thesis that secularisation is an historical product of Christianity requires a much more thorough historical investigation. He points out that "Western culture is a complex of elements. The Greco-Roman as well as the Judaeo-Christian went into its making. The tension between the two traditions will have produced results inexplicable by either alone. Account, too, must be taken of the natural dynamism of human intelligence. Limited as man is by his environment, individual genius can still introduce new factors, which go on to have incalculable effects. Further, it is possible to maintain that secularisation would not have taken place in the West without the presence of Christianity, while at the same time denying its Christian character. A factor in a given situation may provoke a reaction inimical to itself. On the other hand, to judge a cultural development as advantageous to Christian progress is not to prove that Christianity was its cause. It is a well-known characteristic of the Christian faith to profit from each new historical situation imposed upon it and under external stimulus to display fresh potentialities" (pp. 19-20). Davis's remarks seem to me to be eminently sensible; they sound a note of warning against too easily assuming that secularisation is essentially Christian. Moreover, we need to distinguish between the theoretical assumptions upon which techniques are built and the use to which they may be put. While it may be true that the technology of the West rests upon a desacralisation of nature it does not follow that mass production techniques are used in accordance with the Gospel. We know all too well that their use often results in dehumanisation, in making a man a mere cog in a machine. In other words his creation in the image of God is ignored. Cox and others scarcely notice the evil effects of secularisation in their desire to stress its positive achievements. In Cox's theology, which he claims is biblical, there is no room either for Babel (Gen. 11), "the godless society", or for the holy city which comes "down out of heaven" (Rev. 21:10, 24, 27). He cannot see that technology may well be producing a Babel, and that it is certainly not bringing in the eternal order. He shows no awareness of books like the late Rachel Carson's *The Silent Spring,* which demonstrate how technological man is maltreating nature in the interests of the mass-production of food. Nor does he seem to have pondered the significance of such books as Vance Packard's *The Hidden Persuaders,* which shows the way in which modern communications techniques are being used to persuade people to buy commodities they do not need.

Cox sees as the third mark of secular society what he calls the *deconsecration of values.* By this he means that modern secular man realises that his values are relative. He writes, "The awareness that his own point of view is relative and conditioned has become for secular man an inescapable component of that point of view. His consciousness has been relativised. He knows that not only his language, his customs and his clothing style, but also his science, his values, and his way of perceiving reality are conditioned by his personal biography and the history of his group" (p. 30). Cox sees this relativism as stemming in principle from the prohibition against "graven images" which was part of the Sinai Covenant. "It means," writes Cox, "that the Jews were forbidden to worship (that is, to take with any real moral seriousness) anything fashioned by man himself . . . it was because they believed in Yahweh that, for the Jews, all human values and their representations were relativised" (p. 32).

But while what Cox says is true negatively, he gives us no real clue as to how we may be saved from the morass of subjectivism. True he is aware of the danger (pp. 33-36) but he cannot meet it with a positive answer, as the following sentence shows: "There is no reason that man must believe the ethical standards he lives by came down from heaven on golden tablets" (p. 35). This may be true of an individual's own ethical code but the real question is "Has anything come down from heaven?". In other words, is there a God-given revelation which will serve as a norm of judgment? Is there a body of truth by which all of men's standards may be judged? The trouble with Cox is that he wants to appeal to the Sinai Covenant as originating the deconsecration of values whilst avoiding the questions, "Did God speak there? Was His word understood correctly? Was it recorded accurately?" But one cannot avoid such questions, especially when one writes, "Historical relativism is the end product of secularisation" (p. 33). The biblical revelation was given in history.

Is it therefore relative? Cox would answer "Yes". As biblical Christians we cannot accept Cox's position. Rather we find ourselves in agreement with the words of Rousas J. Rushdoony: "In terms of Scripture we must insist that because God created all things, the full circle of meaning exists only where He is accepted as both creator and interpreter of reality. And these principles of interpretation come only from an inspired and authoritative Scripture. Ultimately, therefore, all knowledge and not merely knowledge of God, hinges on the doctrine of inspiration which accordingly is not peripheral but central to Christian faith. The alternative is the blind reaches of subjectivity and nihilism" (*By What Standard?* p. 140).

From the foregoing discussion the following questions suggest themselves: How far is secularisation an effect of the Gospel, and how far have other factors played their part? Is it possible to draw a sharp distinction between secularisation and secularism? How far is secularisation a process of dechristianisation?

Now I do not propose to attempt an answer to these questions, although the lines along which I would do so will have already become explicit. What I would say is that these and other related questions are ones with which we should be wrestling. If we would be the bearers of the Gospel to our times we cannot ignore them.

What then are the marks of the secular mind? I would suggest that the secular mind is characterised by four marks.

Firstly, it is *autonomous*. This is another way of saying that secular man is no different from men since Eden, a fact which all talk of man's "coming of age" overlooks. Rushdoony's words are as applicable to secular man as pre-secular man. "The temptation of man is 'To be as God', knowing, that is, determining for himself what shall be good and what shall be evil. Man establishes his own law and decrees his own righteousness and is not bound to a point of reference beyond himself" (op. cit., p. 5). Autonomous man lives in God's world, yet he seeks to push God out of it, to the very borders of his existence, and even beyond. Thus the secular scientist assumes that he can find an empirical explanation for every natural phenomenon. With Laplace he says that he has no need of the God-hypothesis to complete his explanation of observable reality. The exclusion of the Creator from His creation comes to the clearest expression in the following statement of Sir Julian Huxley: "God can no longer be considered as the controller of the universe in any but a Pickwickian sense. The God-hypothesis is no longer of any pragmatic value for the interpretation or comprehension of nature, and indeed often stands in the way of better and truer interpretation. Operationally, God is beginning to resemble not a ruler, but the last fading smile of a cosmic Cheshire cat" (quoted David H. Freeman: *A Philosophical Study of Religion*, p 159).

The second characteristic of the secular mind is that it is *antisupernaturalistic*. In principle it secularises everything by denying the supernatural altogether. Thus secular man believes neither in God, revelation, the incarnation, miracles, angels, demons, heaven or hell. Huxley, to quote him again, says, "I submit that the discoveries of physiology, general biology and psychology not only make possible but necessitate a naturalistic hypothesis, in which there is no room for the supernatural . ." (quoted by Freeman, *ibid.*, p. 159). Modern secular man lives in a closed world, a world which is shut against the revelation of one who, while immanent, is also transcendent. Those theologians who seek to accommodate the Gospel to secular man therefore tend to deny the transcendence of God by interpreting it in immanent terms. Thus Bishop Robinson reduces theology to anthropology and therefore turns transcendence into immanence when he writes that "theological statements are not a description of 'the highest Being' but an analysis of the depths of personal relationships—or, rather, an analysis of the depths of all experience 'interpreted by love'. Theology, as Tillich insists, is about 'that which concerns us ultimately'. A statement is 'theological' not because it relates to a particular Being called 'God', but because it asks ultimate questions about the meaning of existence; it asks what, at the level of theos, at the level of its deepest mystery, is the reality and significance of our life" (*Honest to God*, p. 49).

Thirdly, the secular mind is *this-worldly*. As Harry Blamires puts it in his little masterpiece of contemporary apologetics, *The Christian Mind*, "To think secularly is to think within a framework bounded by the limits of our life on earth, it is to keep one's calculations rooted in this worldly criteria" (p. 44). Thus the secular mind is pragmatic. It emphasises function and ignores value. It is empirical. "Its most basic presupposition implicit in all its judgments," writes Blamires, "is that this which we experience directly with the senses constitutes the heart and totality of things. Hence the collision between the Christian faith and contemporary secular culture" (p. 68).

Lastly, the secular mind is *antiauthoritarian*. Whilst this has its good aspects, *e.g.* the struggle against totalitarianism, yet in its totality the antiauthoritarian temper of the secular mind is inimical to the Christian faith. For the Christian faith presupposes the authority of God, then the authority of His revelation through prophet, priest and His incarnate Son, His commandments and His Church. The secular mind, in its refusal to live under the authority of God, recognises only the authority of the individual self, which is why hedonism is the popular philosophy of our times.

These, then, are the marks of the secular mind. It is *autonomous* and thus it cannot interpret reality aright, for in a world created by God He it is who provides the true interpretation of this world to man.

It is *antisupernaturalistic*, and so it is a closed world, into which God is not permitted to come. Therefore statements about God are no more, in fact, than statements about man.

It is *this-worldly*, so man no longer lives "sub specie aetemitatis". The world of secular man, the world he sees, is the only world. And so, in principle, secular man has no eschatology, for he has no room in his thinking for the last things. As he denies the biblical doctrine of creation so he denies the eschatology of the Bible.

Finally it is *antiauthoritarian*. Thus secular man can believe in love, but not in power. He cannot therefore believe in divine Fatherhood, "benign yet authoritative, loving yet powerful, merciful yet wrathful" (Blamires, p. 140).

In the light of these characteristics of the secular mind we can see the appropriateness of Friedrich Gogarten's definition of secularisation: "human existence comes to be determined by the dimensions of time and history" (quoted Arend Th. van Leeuwen: *Christianity in World History,* p. 331).

2. The Development of Secular Thinking

It is obviously impossible, within the limits of a single paper, to do justice to the changes which have taken place in secular thinking since the Renaissance, which I shall make my starting-point. So I am obliged to be selective and thematic in my treatment. Therefore I shall run the risk of over-simplifying issues, and of distorting the history of intellectual movements. But the risk has to be taken.

It is impossible to treat secular thinking in isolation from secular society. When we speak of secular society we are, of course, speaking of the West, for it is in the Christian West that the process historians call secularisation has taken place. We should, however, keep before us the fact that the West, through the adoption of Western scientific ideas and techniques, is in process of secularising the East. Therefore, any strategy of mission which may be developed for the secularised West, will also have considerable relevance for the mission of the Christian Church in the East.

When we say that secular thinking cannot be treated in isolation from secular society we mean that it must be related to economics, politics, technology, sociology. We must, therefore, first of all, examine the development of secular society. Then against the background of our understanding of it, we must set those intellectual movements of modern history which can more strictly be viewed as exemplifying "secular thinking".

(a) *The Secular Society.*

In the later middle-ages, from the 13th century onwards, towns began to re-appear after a decline which had lasted since the breakdown of the Roman Empire in the 4th and 5th centuries A.D. The religious and cultural movement which we call the Renaissance, which took place in the 14th and 15th centuries, would have been inconceivable without the growth of commerce associated with the towns. And town culture is familiar to us all, for as Harvey Cox says, "The age of the towns gave us printing and books, rational theology, the scientific revolution, investment capitalism, and bureaucracy" (p. 13).

But we no longer live in the age of the town, we live in the age of the city and the metropolis. Thus a leading feature of our culture is *urbanisation*. Man is being gathered in larger and larger units. He plans and builds new cities, in which he is subject to a degree of bureaucratic organisation never known before. In the city he is *mobile* man, whose home and place of work are separated. In the city he is *anonymous* man, whose identity is lost in the crowd of which he is an insignificant part. While he is dependent upon a large number of people for services, urban man can only afford to be interested in a few people as individuals. He therefore distinguishes sharply between his public and private life. He comes home "to forget the office"; he weekends "to get away from *it* (a significant word, suggesting the impersonality of the city) all", in company with a few chosen companions. Urban man is also mobile man, in that he moves from job to job, especially if he belongs to the scientific or managerial élite. As he moves up, so he tends to move from one class to another, and therefore from one neighbourhood to another.

The phenomenon of urbanisation is the context in which secular man lives. It is in this context that the Church must exercise its mission today. It is doubtful whether most evangelicals have yet realised that they are living in the age of urbanisation, for their churches give the appearance of being still geared to village or town conditions. Thus, in Africa today, despite the rapidly growing cities, the greater proportion of missionary activity is centred in the countryside, with the result that the new proletariat and the new intelligentsia are being neglected in

59

evangelism. Some American writers, Gibson Winter in particular, speak on the other hand, referring to a different urban context, of the "suburban captivity of the churches" with its invariable concomitant, the abandonment of the inner city. Anyone who knows how evangelical churches have declined in inner London and yet flourish in the outer suburbs will agree that his analysis is just.

Urbanisation could not have taken place without industrialisation, for urbanisation could not have taken place without the Industrial and the Technical Revolutions. Both these Revolutions, of course, presuppose the Scientific Revolution, which for purposes of convenience we may say began with Galileo (1564-1642).

Secular man is confident in his power to solve every problem. He sees the application of theoretical science (technology) as capable of bringing him a better life, with a greater variety of experiences, that only 50 years ago would have been thought impossible. His faith is not in God. It is in "science", as he calls it—that is, in technology. He has no place in his thinking for revelation, since "reason", applied to life through technology, has brought him more money, a reduction in the hours he works with a consequent increase in his leisure-time. Added to which he lives longer due to the progress of medical science. To secular man God seems irrelevant, for he insists that his hands have made his world a better place in which to live. So he has no sense of being a stranger on the earth, of being on a short, uncertain earthly pilgrimage. He lives in an improving world in which the speed of change is ever accelerating. The eternal order is not a subject for contemplation because he has subsumed heaven under the reference of "earth". He is "this-worldly", for the technological age is based on "this-worldly" premises.

Furthermore, secular man lives in an expanding universe. He knows more of the world in which he lives than any of his predecessors. Modern media of communication bring the world's history, culture and happenings to his fireside. His grandfather twiddled a cat's-whisker; he *sees* what is happening on the other side of the world via a communications satellite. He is aware of other cultures, other faiths, than the Christian culture and faith of the Western world. To him life on other planets is a real possibility. Why, in a universe, which scientific exploration reveals to be so vast that the earth is like a speck of sand on the ocean's shore, should life be confined to the world we know? And he knows that, invisible to his naked eye, is the world revealed by the electron microscope—a world of atoms, neutrons, protons. And why should not man, he asks, discover the secret of life, and create life? And if he can do this—and secular man does not really doubt that he will—where is there room for the Creator?

Now if we fail to appreciate the theological significance of urbanisation and of the technological revolution, which is really only just beginning, we shall fail to preach the everlasting Gospel in a way which is truly relevant. What then is the theological significance of urbanisation and the Technological Revolution?

First, I believe that they have resulted in making secular man *unable to contemplate.* Modern production techniques, by the speed at which they require a man to work, and by the smallness of the part which they allow him to play in the making of any product, mean that he has no time to stop and think and contemplate the work of his own hands. This is reflected in the fact that modern man must be mobile, that he cannot bear silence, so he fills it with the noise of a radio or a television set. Modern man simply would not say with the psalmist, "For God alone my soul *waits* in *silence*; from Him comes my salvation" (Psa. 62:1 R.S.V.).

Second, secular man has no sense of *transcendence.* This fact is related to the former, for one only contemplates when one believes in a transcendent order. Modern secular man has no sense of transcendent purpose. He does not know what he is here for. He does not know what is the purpose of his life, for the technological age in which he lives concentrates on the question "how", to the neglect of the question "why". He is here to earn wages, but "how" only concerns him. He is here to possess things, but their use raises no ethical questions for him. And for this reason: that his life has no reference to the transcendent realm. Therefore the vision of God, eternity, heaven and hell are not concepts he knows. They just do not matter to him.

Because of his confidence in technology secular man has *no sense of dependence.* He is not aware of this creatureliness to any significant degree. He is confident of his ability to solve by research, planning and organisation any problems which remain. The God of the Bible, infinite in power and holiness, is therefore anathema to modern man, for He obliges him to confess his creatureliness and to recognise his corruption, and this he will not do.

(b) *The rise of modern science.*

Whilst we must not abstract secular man from his context in secular society we must not, on the other hand, fall into the error of supposing that man is entirely the product of his environment. To take this position is to deny the dynamism of human intelligence; it is to deny the pioneer thinking of gifted men and women and the ability of man to shape his surroundings.

Well before the Renaissance, as Lagarde has shown, a lay spirit manifested itself in the cities of Northern Italy, Southern France and Germany. City life was emancipated from clerical domination. In the towns, for the first time since classical antiquity, lay schools arose. The use of the vernacular in writing, and the growth of a vernacular literature were

61

prominent in medieval town culture. It was this lay spirit which came fully into its own during the Renaissance. Whilst one must be cautious in generalising about the Renaissance, for it was a complex and many-sided movement, some generalisations are in order. During the Renaissance there was a re-discovery of the literature and some of the philosophy of classical antiquity. In consequence, especially in Italy, there was a revival of paganism. Whilst traditional Christian doctrines were not denied, there was nevertheless a shifting of emphasis from God to man, from grace to nature. Thus it is correct to speak of Renaissance humanism. Rightly interpreted the Renaissance was, in the words of Herman Dooyeweerd "a religious movement, aiming at a transformation of the Christian religion into a religion of human personality and of humanity" (*In the Twilight of Western Thought,* p. 65).

The extent of the influence of the Renaissance upon the Reformation is still a matter for considerable scholarly debate. But when we remember that Luther, and especially Calvin, and even more so Melanchthon, and a host of other Reformers, were influenced by Renaissance humanism, we shall be disposed to allow that its influence was considerable. The Reformers did not see the Renaissance as an enemy, but rather as a friend. Thus though religiously the Reformers turned their backs upon the synergism of Renaissance theology they accepted the Renaissance concern for exact historical scholarship and interest in a rational form of the Church.

The Reformation, especially in its Calvinistic aspect, encouraged the growth of science, for it broke down the division between sacred and secular, by insisting that under God's sovereignty the believer should glorify Him in his calling. The Calvinistic doctrine of vocation made the pursuit of scientific enquiry as honourable in the sight of God as the preaching of the Word of God.

The extent to which Calvinism fostered the growth of capitalism is again a matter for scholarly debate, but it would be idle to deny that there is a very definite relationship between the two. Because it dignified work as an ordinance of God, and viewed thrift and sobriety as positive virtues, Calvinism encouraged the growth of capitalism. But I think that the chief reason why it did so is stated by van Leeuwen: "The fundamental reason why Calvinism was so important to the rise of modern capitalism is that it concerned itself in a positive way with the implications of an urban money economy" (p. 310). Which is, of course, not to say that Calvinism originated usury!

The 17th century is pivotal in our survey, for in that century modern science, as distinct from ancient and medieval science, may be said to have emerged. Of crucial importance was the development of mathematics, and particularly the invention of calculus by Sir Isaac Newton (1642-1727). In the rise of modern science in the 17th century the key feature according to Ian G. Barbour was "the new combination of mathematical reasoning and experimental observation" (*Issues in Science and Religion,* p. 23). This combination is exemplified in the work of Galileo (1564-1642) who has been rightly called the father of modern science. What is especially important is that Galileo did not ask *why,* for example, objects fall, but *how* they fall. "Teleological explanation, characteristic of earlier thought, had given way to descriptive explanation" (Barbour, p. 26). This approach is characteristic of modern science. Interest is not directed to the part a phenomenon plays in an all-embracing metaphysical system, but to a description of *how* it is produced.

Sir Isaac Newton (1642-1727) was even more insistent than Galileo that the scientist's task is descriptive, and that speculation about ultimate issues was to be avoided. Newton's laws of motion and gravity seemed to be applicable to all objects from the smallest particle to the farthest planet. The world was, to his mind, mathematical in structure. This suggested the image of the world as an intricate machine following immutable laws, with every detail precisely predictable. The image of the world as a machine gave rise to an elaborate metaphysics in which God was progressively banished to the periphery of life. God became the divine Clockmaker, who was needed only to make the clock, and to start it going, but not to maintain its motion. Newton, it is true, called on God to make any necessary adjustments in the solar system, but Leibniz was to point out the theological inadequacy of such a view: a perfect God would not have created an imperfect mechanism requiring periodic correction. We have, by now, arrived at the "God of the gaps", a concept so rightly criticised by Bishop Robinson. The "God of the gaps" was introduced to explain areas yet closed to scientific knowledge, but He is always in retreat since the gaps are continually being filled as scientific knowledge advances. So He becomes in Barbour's phrase, the Retired Architect.

The 18th century has been labelled the Age of Reason. This is not a strictly accurate description, since it was also the age of Romanticism and of the Evangelical Awakening. But it is certainly true that in France most notably, but also in Germany, England, and the American colonies, there was an unbounded confidence in the power of reason. Three concepts of the Enlightenment are particularly relevant to our survey. Firstly nature was viewed as a self-sufficient, self-sustaining deterministic mechanism whose operation could be explained by natural forces. Secondly, God became a debatable hypothesis, whose existence or non-existence was a matter for argument. Thirdly, man was held to be perfectible and the achievement of an ideal society was held to be possible by the application of reason to human affairs. In this connection it is no accident that the late 18th and 19th centuries saw the publication of many diverse visions of Utopia.

In the 19th century the pace of scientific discovery dramatically quickened. Physics expanded with theories about light, electricity and thermodynamics. New scientific concepts were employed, such as interacting fields and statistical probabilities. Chemistry was enlarged by the formulation of Dalton's atomic theory early in the century to Mendeleer's formulation of the periodic table and the rise of organic chemistry by its close. But the most far-reaching advance was made in the field of biology. The name associated with it is, of course, that of Charles Darwin. Darwin's theory of natural selection brought about a direct conflict between science and religion. Firstly, it challenged the still popular argument from design. This argument started from what could be observed, namely, the adaptation of organic structures to useful functions. But such an adaptation could now be explained, it seemed, by the concept of natural selection, without recourse to the idea of a preconceived plan. Usefulness was no longer viewed as a cause but as an effect, the end-product of an impersonal process.

Secondly, Darwin's theory of natural selection challenged man's unique status, for Darwin and his followers minimised the differences between human and animal characteristics. Huxley claimed that the difference between man and the highest apes was less great than that between the higher and lower apes.

Thirdly, Darwin's theory challenged the assumption that ethics are given from without, for he tried to derive ethical values from the evolutionary process. "There should be open competition for all men; and the most able should not be prevented by laws or customs from succeeding best and rearing the largest number of offspring." With such a statement we start on the road to the experiments in eugenics which were a feature of Hitler's Germany.

When the concept of natural selection was wedded to the idea of progress as in the philosophy of Herbert Spencer a secularised version of the doctrine of providence was the result. As Barbour says, "Faith in progress replaced the doctrines of creation and providence as assurance that the universe is not really purposeless" (p. 94).

In the 20th century the destructive use to which scientific discoveries have been put has created for many scientists a new awareness of the ethical implications of their work. Many scientists are now openly admitting that man cannot control himself. They are pleading for a return to a religious view of the universe. But they are shut up in an impasse, for they want to maintain the autonomy of human reason. Thus they lack the key to the true interpretation of reality, for only as man listens to and submits to the Word of God does he find the "key to true self-knowledge in its dependency on the true knowledge of God" (Dooyeweerd, p. 186). Modern scientific man is reaping the bitter fruit of Adam's desire to be as God. He has within his hands power which could obliterate humanity, but he cannot solve the problem of his own existence. Thus he lies under the judgment of God; without God he cannot be truly man until he knows Him as a regenerate sinner.

(c) *The rise of non-Christian world views.*

It is simpler to consider the movements in philosophy in connection with the rise of non-Christian world views, than to isolate philosophy as a single field of study. It is so for this reason: that any world view is based upon certain philosophical assumptions, yet it tends to draw to itself concepts from other sciences. Thus Marxism is based upon the concept of dialectical materialism but it also draws material from economic theory and from what would today be called sociology.

(i) *Marxism.*

Marxism is, in origin, an entirely Western phenomenon, although in the form of Leninism and Maoism it has had its greatest success outside the West.

Marx grasped the importance of the 19th century proletarian revolution as no other thinker of his time did. He saw the importance of the emergence of the large class of wage-slaves which he designated the proletariat. "The really significant thing about Marxism," writes van Leeuwen, "was that it responded to the challenge of the proletarian revolution, pronouncing it to be a necessary stage in the evolution of Western society" (p. 333).

From Hegel, Marx took the dialectical view of world history—thesis, antithesis—synthesis—and transformed historical idealism into historical materialism. From Feuerbach he borrowed the idea that religion was a projection of man, and added to it the concept of its being the product of social relationships. Thus religion is the opiate of the people, designed by capitalistic entrepreneurs, to dull the senses of the exploited proletariat. Marx, as has often been remarked, stands, in terms of passion, in the line of the Hebrew prophets, especially Amos. Truth for him was inseparable from its consequences in action. He believed in *doing* truth. "The philosophers," he once said, "have only interpreted the world in one way or another; the thing now is to change it."

Marxism is a *world* view, for it claims to provide the key to the interpretation of history. It is teleological for it views economic development as moving towards a predetermined end. It is eschatological, for it looks for a new heaven and a new earth, inaugurated by the day of the Lord which the proletariat ushers in. "This," van Leeuwen aptly suggests, "is a secularised biblical eschatology in which the proletariat has assumed

65

the broad features of the Servant of the Lord, whose vicarious suffering for the whole creation inaugurates the new age" (p. 338).

Lenin modified Marxism to meet the Russian situation. In Russia before the Revolution in 1917 there was no capitalistic middle-class of any consequence, so Lenin simply skipped the period of capitalism. The Russian people, a nation of labourers and peasants, were identified with the industrial proletariat of Marx's analysis, and Russian Messianism was merged with the Messianism of the proletariat.

Marxism, which was formulated in England, the then most industrially advanced country of the world, has proved itself to be extremely adaptable. It has taken root in countries with little or no industry, such as China and Cuba. It now is the official creed of about one third of the world's population. It must be taken seriously for it presents a world view which provides, for many people it seems, a satisfying interpretation of history and life. It must be met, not by a blanket defence of the Western way of life, but by an assault upon its underlying presuppositions.

(ii) *Naturalism.*
Naturalism might be defined as the transference of the biblical doctrine of God to the realm of nature. Thus nature is regarded as self-creating and self-ordering. The "laws of nature", so called, are not viewed as demanding a law-giver. They may be investigated without any reference to the Creator, on the assumption that since the world is wholly governed by natural causes, a "deus ex machina" is not required to fill in any gaps that there may be in our knowledge of the world. Naturalism is probably the most dominant world view of our time. For example, in everyday speech it is said, "Nature arranges it this way", or "This or that is Nature's way of doing things".

There are various types of naturalism: we shall glance at the three main types.

First, there is *materialistic naturalism.* Materialistic naturalism is represented in the thought of the German zoologist, Ernst Haeckel. (It is sometimes called evolutionary monism.) Haeckel in his best known book *The Riddle of the Universe* maintained that matter and force are the only ultimate reality. Haeckel was supremely confident that the new biology explained everything: "The cell consists of matter called protoplasm, composed chiefly of carbon with an admixture of hydrogen, nitrogen and sulphur. These component parts properly united produce the soul and body of the animated world, and suitably nursed become man. *With this single argument* the mystery of the universe is explained, the Deity annulled, and a new era of infinite knowledge ushered in" (quoted Barbour, p. 109).

The basic assumption of materialism is that whatever exists is of the same sort as matter. The thinking of the materialist has no room for the operation of non-physical forces. His universe has no place for a God who is Spirit, nor for a man who is more than the sum total of the chemistry of his body.

Materialistic naturalism may take either an optimistic or a pessimistic form. When allied with Marxism it takes on an optimistic line because of the underlying Messianism of Marxism. Thus the Marxist believes in a "day of the Lord" when the state will have withered away, and the dictatorship of the proletariat will no longer be needed. On the other hand, nature can be viewed as purposeless, as being utterly indifferent to the interests of man. Then one either lapses into despair or stoic resignation, or one fights back with Promethean defiance. Bertrand Russell displays the spirit of Prometheus when he writes: "Man is the product of causes which had no prevision of the end they were achieving; his origin, his growth, his hopes and fears, his loves and his beliefs, are but the outcome of accidental collocations of atoms . . . Blind to good and evil, reckless of destruction, omnipotent matter rolls on its relentless way . . . It is for Man, proudly defiant of the irresistible forces that tolerate for a moment his knowledge and his condemnation to sustain alone, a weary but unyielding Atlas, the world that his own ideals have fashioned despite the trampling march of unconscious power" (quoted Barbour, p. 110).

In the thought of Friedrich Nietzsche materialistic naturalism is employed to invert the moral order. Nietzsche accepted the Darwinian doctrine of the survival of the fittest, and employed it against traditional ethics. In the struggle for survival self-assertion and the will to power are good, whilst humility, love and pity are bad, for they are a morality fit for slaves. The Nietzschean hero is above law, not subject to it; he is or should be free from every moral scruple. With his concept of the Superman Nietzsche deified power, helping thus to sow some of the seeds of the Nazi ideology.

A second form of naturalism may be described as *evolutionary naturalism*. A leading representative of this type of naturalism is Julian Huxley. In contrast to Haeckel Huxley is willing to recognise the emergence of qualitatively new levels of existence. He is also deeply concerned about human life and social values.

While Huxley postulates man's continuity with lower forms he also appreciates the uniqueness of man. He feels that there is a trend in the world "toward sentience, mind and richness of being, operating so widely but so sparsely in the cosmos" (quoted Barbour, p. 409). He feels that this provides a basis for a naturalistic religion, an evolution-centred faith in man's values and capabilities. He attempts to derive ethical norms from evolution. His definition of good is of an evolutionary concept.

67

"Anything which permits or promotes open development is right; anything which frustrates development is wrong" (quoted Barbour, p. 410). Huxley's definition of good emphasises the abyss into which all naturalistic systems of ethics plunge, namely, tautology. Development is good because it is development, is what Huxley is saying. But why is development good? Because it is development.

The fact of the matter is that ethical principles cannot be derived from nature; they must come from "outside" of nature. But Huxley's evolutionary naturalism will not allow him to admit this, because to do so would be to say that science cannot solve all problems, for it cannot be the source of ethical norms.

A third type of naturalism may be described as *psychological*. In this type religion particularly receives a naturalistic interpretation. Since this interpretation is often believed to have scientific support it behoves us to examine it with some care.

In the 19th century Ludwig Feuerbach, as we have already mentioned, claimed that the idea of God is a product of man's imagination, a personification of his needs and a rationalisation of his desires. "Gods are the wishes of men represented as real beings. God is nothing but man's desire for happiness, satisfied in imagination" (quoted Barbour, p. 255).

It is due to the works of Sigmund Freud that the naturalistic interpretation of religion has become part of the ideas of our time. Freud explained theism as the product of a subconscious father-complex. Every child is helpless and dependent on his human father. (But is the child not even more dependent upon his mother? If this is so, why is not theism to be explained as the product of an unconscious mother-complex?) As the child grows to maturity he realises that he cannot be for ever dependent upon his father. So in a hostile world, in his constant insecurity, he imagines a divine being who is an image of his father projected on a cosmic scale, to which he can turn for comfort and strength.

Now while what Freud believed may be true of some religions, it is quite another thing to argue that it is true of all. It is certainly going beyond the verifiable data to make this assumption. The Christian religion is not wish-fulfilment when it makes demands that run clean counter to natural desires. Taking up the cross is hardly describable as a projection of basic desires. The truth or falsity of a belief can never be decided by assuming its relation to human wishes. For instance, it does not follow that because we want to feel secure, that the Christian belief in the active providence of God is therefore no more than a projection of a man's desire for assurance. As Barbour says "The validity of a belief can neither be proved nor disproved from its psychological origins or motives alone". Furthermore, Freud's own argument can be turned against him. Why should not his atheism equally be the projection, for example, of his desire to be free from parental control?

The truth of the matter is that Freud's claim to be objective and scientific in his analysis of religion is false, for his writing reveals a naturalistic world view. He selects what agrees with it, and ignores what does not, preferring to draw his examples from pathological cases or from primitive religion. His interpretation of religion in fact rests upon a prior commitment to presuppositions which are hostile to the Christian world-view, but which he did not, nor could, establish by scientific experimentation. Freud is a man of faith, not in the God of the Bible, but in the religious pre-suppositions which govern his thinking.

I conclude this section of my paper with a brief mention of two types of philosophical outlook which are popular today. One type, existentialism, has been and is very influential on the Continent of Europe. The other, logical positivism, or, as it is now usually called, linguistic analysis, has exercised and still does a profound influence in university circles in both Great Britain and the United States of America. It is worth noting that the former in the form promulgated by Martin Heidegger, is the basis on which Rudolf Bultmann has sought to re-interpret the Gospel by means of what he calls demythologisation. On the other hand, Paul van Buren in his book *The Secular Meaning of the Gospel* attempts to accommodate the Gospel to the thinking of modern man by the use of the tool of linguistic analysis. So while these two philosophical systems, existentialism and linguistic analysis, may seem of academic interest only, they are in fact being used as instruments in the fashioning of a Gospel which is not the Gospel of the New Testament.

Existentialism is perhaps better described as an attitude rather than as a system of thought. In essence it makes man the measure of all things, for in all its forms it asserts that we can know authentic human existence only by being personally involved as concrete individuals making free decisions—not by formulating abstract general ideas or universal laws about man. Thus when an existentialist like Bultmann (or for that matter Barth, in many instances) comes to Scripture he interprets what he reads as being always in some sense a statement about my personal existence and my personal relationship to God. Thus, for example, the Fall is not a fact of history. It never happened *in* time, but is rather a statement about man, *i.e.* he *is* fallen. Thus "Adam is everyman" (Richardson). To select another example, the resurrection was not, according to Bultmann, a physical event, but rather an occurrence in the experience of the early Church, the return of faith in Christ, which was probably originated by an hallucination!

Linguistic analysis is concerned with the analysis of the way in which language is used in various fields of discourse. Thus the linguistic philosopher will ask, Is the statement "God exists" of the same kind as the statement "that rose is red"? The slogan of the linguistic philosopher is "Don't ask about the meaning of a statement; ask about its use".

Now from these brief remarks it should be obvious that both existentialism and linguistic analysis present serious challenges to the Christian faith. Existentialism does so because it severs the Gospel from history, linguistic analysis because it tacitly assumes that the truth of the Gospel is of no real importance.

3. The mission of biblical Christianity in a secular world

How is biblical Christianity to be communicated to modern, secular man? What particular biblical doctrines are of especial relevance as this task is undertaken?

I would begin by underlining the fact that the testimony of the Church which claims to be biblical includes the books of the Old Testament. This is extremely important, since in practice much evangelical witness today is sadly impoverished due to the neglect of the study and preaching of the Old Testament. But without a clear understanding of the Old Testament, especially of what it teaches about idolatry, no New Testament Church can have an adequate answer to secular thinking.

Now I shall not attempt to offer a programme suggesting *how* the adequate answer that we believe we have shall be proclaimed by the Church. Our situations vary so much that it would be foolish to presume to tell you how you must go about your task. What I propose to do is to suggest some principles which may guide action.

(a) *The sovereignty of God must be declared.*
By this I do not mean that *every* sermon is to set forth the five points of Calvinism; despite what some think there is more in the Bible than that! But what I do mean is that the testimony of each local church must have as its great presupposition the glorious truth of the sovereignty of God. The God the Bible reveals to us is sovereign, free, unconditioned. He is the Creator, sustainer and ruler of the world. He is the living Lord to whom man is called to be subject in filial love.

The tragedy of modern man is that he tries to live in God's world without God. His thinking is built upon the premise that his science, his technology, his bureaucracy, his politics, can be constructed as though God did not exist. And so he comes to the position where he can proclaim as the Gospel that God is dead! He is so irrelevant that His existence no longer matters.

Now I am persuaded that the testimony of a local church must challenge secular man's rejection of God's sovereignty.

1. We must do so, firstly, by insisting that the sovereignty of God extends to every area of life. There is nowhere where His writ does not run (Psa. 139).

What does this mean in practical terms? It means that we do not allow ourselves, or the non-Christian, to divide life into two compartments, religious and secular. Life is *one* because our sovereign God is one, though triune. It is rebellion on the part of man to protest, for example, that religion should not be brought into politics. If a Christian thinks as a Christian how can he help bringing religion into politics? Is not God concerned with political aims?

It is my conviction that the Bible will not permit us to divide life into ecclesiastical and worldly compartments. It is a mark of man's rebellion that he seeks to confine God in an ever-decreasing compartment. After he fell into sin Adam tried to hide from the presence of the Lord (Gen. 3:8), an act of folly that is continually being repeated. Secular man can only be understood as hiding from God when he tries to push Him out of the world altogether.

The weakness of much evangelism is due to the fact that it accepts without question the compartmentalising of life, and so it in effect fights its battles on ground chosen by secular man. Thus it concerns itself only with the soul, as if the Gospel had nothing to say about the body. Or it assumes that the Bible has nothing to say about how our children are to be educated, so it permits their education to be carried out in schools founded on a philosophy of education which is in absolute conflict with the Christian faith. Until contemporary evangelicalism recovers the profound sense of the sovereignty of God which the Puritans, for example, had, it will not make any real impact upon the secular world.

2. Secondly, we must challenge secular man's rejection of God's sovereignty by insisting that nothing can be properly interpreted out of relation to God.

The God of the Bible "works all things after the counsel of His own will" (Eph. 1:11)—not some things, or most things, but *all* things. He is the one "of whom and through whom, and to whom all things, to whom be glory for ever" (Rom. 11:36). For His pleasure and glory all things have been created (Rev. 4:11).

There is therefore no fact, no event, no thought which can be interpreted without reference to God. God cannot be excluded from the laboratory, from the factory, from the office. Rather all these have their purpose within the sovereign plan of God. It is because secular man has built his life upon the assumption that he can *think* without reference to God that his industry, his town-planning and so on are conducted without so much as even a nod in God's direction.

The testimony of the local church must include within it that which challenges the assumption of secularity—viz. that God can be kept in a religious compartment.

But, positively, it must declare that man can only live in God's world to God's glory as he submits to God's sovereignty. Particularly in the realm of his thinking this means that secular man must be brought to see that it is not he who gives facts their significance, but God. It is not he who is called upon to provide from his mind the key to interpret reality, it is God who has done so in His Word.

3. Man cannot understand God's world without God's Word. Of course, he assumes he can, that what he sees in his test-tube can be understood apart from what God has said in His Word. But that is the measure of his apostasy and it must be challenged as such. When man fell into sin the world was not unaffected; it was brought under the curse. So man cannot understand his existence in the world until he realises that the world as he knows it is not what God intended it to be. As Dooyeweerd has said, man's "apostasy implied the apostasy of the whole temporal world which was concentrated in man's ego. Therefore the earth was cursed, because it had no religious root of its own, but was related to the religious root or centre of human existence" (op. cit., p. 124). He goes on to say: "Thus the central theme of the Holy Scriptures, namely, that of creation, fall into sin, and redemption by Jesus Christ in the communion of the Holy Spirit, has a radical unity of meaning which is related to the central unity of our human existence. It affects the true knowledge of God and ourselves, if our heart is really opened by the Holy Spirit so that it finds itself in the grip of God's Word and has become the prisoner of Jesus Christ. So long as this central meaning of the word revelation is at issue we are beyond the scientific problems both of theology and philosophy" (p. 125).

When secular man looks at this world, which is all he does look at, he cannot find God in it, because although it declares His eternal power and deity, he insists on interpreting it without the Word of God. He will not, to use Calvin's vivid metaphor, put on the spectacles of Scripture, that he might have made clear the indistinct and obscure impressions of God which he receives from the world.

In our testimony we must therefore seek to show secular man that he can neither understand himself, nor the world in which he lives without the Word of God. We must make it clear that from Eden onwards man's constant temptation has been to subject God's Word to his judgment—"So God has actually said?" (Gen. 3:1).

(b) *The pretended autonomy of man must be exposed.*

This task is complementary to the former, for in rejecting God's sovereignty man asserts his own autonomy. The serpent offered man his autonomy: "ye shall be as gods". Here, says Derek Kidner, "is a lie big enough to reinterpret life (this breadth is the power of a false system) and dynamic enough to redirect the flow of affection and ambition. To be as God, and to achieve it by outwitting Him, is an intoxicating programme. God will henceforth be regarded, consciously or not, as rival and enemy".

Secular man thus proceeds on the assumption that he is autonomous. The distinction drawn in medieval Roman Catholic theology between nature and grace helped to make this assumption an unquestioned axiom in the culture of modern man. "By accepting a natural sphere of life, which was supposed to be related to the human intellect alone apart from any religious presupposition, it paved the way for a philosophy which did not acknowledge any other authority than man's human reason" (Dooyeweerd, p. 68). Humanist philosophy later proceeded to eliminate the so-called supernatural sphere, nor would it accept a given world order founded in the divine creation. Thus apostate man sought to think God out of His world.

Now to meet this apostasy it is no use trying to deal with it piecemeal. We must challenge, in the name of Christ, the foundation on which it rests, namely, the autonomy of man. Man was made to live under God's sovereignty, not his own; to love, worship and serve his Creator with all his heart. But the natural man is blinded, he is enslaved by the god of this world. So he knows neither God, himself or the world in which he lives. Without the true knowledge of God he is condemned to pervert his relationships with his fellow men, and to deify the natural order so that it becomes an object of worship, instead of an instrument of homage (Rom. 1:19 ff.). We must therefore challenge man's apostate *thinking* with the proclamation of the full-used message of the biblical revelation. We must realise that our message applies to all of man's life, not just to a private religious sector.

Above all else, we must understand that no man is religiously neutral; he is either a natural man or a spiritual man, that is, he is either committed to the presuppositions of autonomous apostate man *or* to the presuppositions of the Gospel of the grace of God. The great divide occurs not between

73

pre-secular and secular man, as Cox, Bonhoeffer and others maintain, but between unregenerate and regenerate man. If a man is unregenerate he is committed to a world-view which in *principle* (although the degree may vary from individual to individual, and from one cultural period to another) rules out God because it is founded on the presupposition of the autonomy of man. Likewise if a man is regenerate, he is, in principle, committed to a world-view which is determined by the Scriptural revelation, a world created, governed *and interpreted* by the One of whom, through whom, and to whom, are all things. The regenerate man, in accord with this fact, judges, or discerns, *"all things"* (I Cor. 2:15). His judgment is not confined to the so called spiritual sphere of the church and the Christian life. He judges "all things", that is, the whole of life as he knows it and experiences it, because the Spirit by the Word gives him the only true norm of judgment.

When we understand that no man is religiously neutral we shall see to it that our evangelism roots him out of all the intellectual bolt-holes into which he retreats to escape God. Instead of accepting the demand of the unbelieving scientist that all he wants is *real* proof of the existence of God, we shall seek to show him that he *knows* in his heart that God does exist, but that he is suppressing that truth because of his own ungodliness (Rom. 1:18). Our approach to him will therefore be radical, challenging his claims and exposing their falsity, that the ground might be prepared for the presentation of the truth.

I believe that these two principles, namely, the declaration of God's sovereignty over all persons and things, and the clear understanding of the pretended autonomy of man, if intelligently and consistently applied will do several things.

1. The assertion of the sovereignty of God will cause us to abandon the pietism which would keep the Church inward looking, concentrating exclusively upon personal soul-culture. It would lead us out, in the name of our sovereign Lord, into the world to call all men to bow the knee and touch the sceptre of His Son. Moreover we would be concerned with the *whole* world of men and affairs for such is the concern of our God, and it is no honour to Him to narrow our vision to ourselves, and to fail to appreciate that the whole of history is ordered by Him.

2. The proper understanding of man's pretended autonomy will enable us to develop a Christian philosophy which because it starts and continues with the biblical view of man presents a world-view which challenges at the deepest level Marxism, scientism, naturalism of various types, existentialism and linguistic philosophy which combine together to form the world-view of secular man.

And let us make no mistake, it is to this task, at various levels of society, and in varying spheres, that the Gospel which we believe most surely commits us.

SELECT BIBLIOGRAPHY

Ian G. Barbour: *Issues in Science and Religion* (S.C.M., 1966).
Paul van Buren: *The Secular Meaning of the Gospel* (S.C.M., Paperback, 1963).
Dietrich Bonhoeffer: *Letters and Papers from Prison* (Fontana, Paperback, 1959).
Harvey Cox: *The Secular City* (S.C.M., Paperback, 1966).
Charles Davis: *God's Grace in History* (Fontana, Paperback, 1966).
Herman Dooyeweerd: *In the Twilight of Western Thought* (Presbyterian and Reformed, 1960).
Arend van Leeuwen: *Christianity in World History* (Edinburgh House Press, 1964).
E. L. Mascall: *The Secularisation of Christianity* (Darton, Longman & Todd P.B., 1965).
John Robinson: *Honest to God* (S.C.M., Paperback, 1963).
Rousas J. Rushdoony: *By What Standard?* (Presbyterian and Reformed, 1959).
Cornelius R. van Til: *The Defence of the Faith* (Paperback revised edition, Presbyterian and Reformed, 1963).
Colin Williams: *Faith in a Secular Age* (Fontana, 1966).
John Bowden and James Richmond (Eds.): *A Reader in Contemporary Theology* (S.C.M., 1967).

THE IMPLICATIONS
of
BIBLICAL THEOLOGY
for our
PREACHING

Jannie du Preez

WE WILL DISCUSS THE FOLLOWING STATEMENTS AND ATTEMPT TO SHOW at least some of their implications for preaching:

1. God has revealed Himself to man.
2. The centre of this revelation is Jesus Christ, the Son of God.
3. Under the inspiration of the Holy Spirit, this revelation has been recorded infallibly in the 66 books of the Bible, by the hands of men.
4. The Bible shows us how this revelation came as salvation history.
5. This salvation history is to be seen as covenant history.
6. Covenant history is a progressive history, basically proceeding from covenant promise in the books of the Old Covenant to covenant fulfilment in the books of the New Covenant.
7. The purpose of this progressive covenant history is the coming of the Kingdom of God.
8. Scripture's Kingdom message to man gives glory to God.

76

I. God has revealed Himself to man.

The so-called God-is-dead-theology is fundamentally a form of doubt with regard to the reality of a *personal* God who has *revealed* Himself to man. In his book *Revolt against Heaven* (1965), Kenneth Hamilton deals with the attacks on the *super-natural* in Christian revelation from the early Gnostics to men like Bishop J. A. T. Robinson. He points out that although these men had the good intention of making the Gospel meaningful to modern man, they tacitly avoided the basic question as to whether our beliefs are a *response to divine revelation*, or whether they are the product of *our own perspective of the universe*.[1] Thus many a modern theologian (like Bultmann) has built something of the sinful self (its so-called scientific world view) into the heart of his theology[2]—a world-view in which there is no place for miracles and least of all for the resurrection of the dead. But the supernatural character of the Gospel is the very issue at stake.[3] The Gospel is a gospel (so Kenneth Hamilton rightly maintains) because it is so much more than the affirmation of what we already know "down here". What flesh and blood could not do, our Father in heaven did: to bring us to the Truth that is in Christ.[4]

The implication for all true preaching is clear: it should rest on the irrefutable conviction that God is a living God who has spoken to man, and is speaking every day. "The Lord God hath spoken, who can but prophesy?" (Amos 3:8). The prophetic "Thus saith the Lord God" should be the watchword of every true sermon. When this conviction lives in the heart of the preacher, he will proclaim in no uncertain terms the *magnalia Dei*, the mighty works of God. The truth will burn upon the preacher's lips, because it has been burned into his soul.[5]

II. The centre of God's revelation to man is Jesus Christ, the Son of God.

Revelation is God's revelation of *Himself* to man. It is therefore *God-centred* in the heart of its matter. And yet, there is a profound sense in which this revelation may be called *Christ*-centred. We may perhaps compare it to a golf ball. We know that every part of its make-up is somehow organically related to the centre. In the same way, every part of God's revelation is somehow organically related to its centre, namely Jesus Christ (cf. Heb. 1:1-4, John 3:16, Acts 4:12, II Cor. 4:6, Gal. 4:4-6).[6] It is the very understanding of the true Christological character of revelation that leads to a true understanding of its God-centred character. For Jesus Christ (who in one person is very God and very man) has come to reveal God to us and bring us back to *Him*. The glory of the Lamb is a God-centred glory. It reveals God's heart and leads to God's throne.[7] It is nothing less than a *trinitarian* glory.[8] For preaching to be truly God-centred, it should be Christ-centred in the above-mentioned sense of the word. Because all the lines of God's revelation have their focal point in Jesus Christ, every sermon should have its focal point in Him too. In every sermon we should somehow behold His glory, "a glory as of the only begotten from the Father, full of grace and truth" (John 1:14).

How this can be the case, will become clearer, I hope, from what will follow.

III. Under the inspiration of the Holy Spirit this revelation of God in Christ has been recorded infallibly in the 66 books of the Bible by the hands of men, for all times to come.

This statement implies a number of others, of which we discuss briefly only the following four:

1. *Firstly, the Bible speaks with divine authority.*

It was part of the deep wisdom of God that He made full use of fallible men to write down an infallible Word, by acting on the writers through His Holy Spirit in an organic way, using them just as they were.[9] Thus, although written by men of flesh and blood, the Bible is a book of divine inspiration, speaking to us with divine authority (II Tim. 3:16-17, II Pet. 1:19-21, Rev. 22:18-19, etc.).

The implication for preaching is clear. All true preaching is the pro-clamation of a divinely authoritative Word. This is a dreadful thing to say, for who are we? And yet, every minister is a *verbi divini minister*, a servant of the divine Word. He is Christ's servant, appointed to pro-claim God's Word in the power of Christ's Spirit.[10]

2. *Secondly, the Bible is a divine unity in diversity.*

There is great variety in the Bible. And yet, it is unmistakably a book of one message: the counsel of the Triune God with Jesus Christ in the centre.

From this unity follow a few important implications for preaching. Apart from the fact that Christ should be seen in all the Scriptures, we mention the following:

(a) *The importance of the immediate context in which a text stands can scarcely be over-emphasised,* and in most cases the old saying will be true: a text without its context is a pretext! We should continually remind people to read and re-read the Bible as if it contains no chapters and no verses. Surely they will often have reason to marvel at the result.

One example must suffice: *Luke 18:8(b).* In the light of the preceding vv. 1-7 (especially v. 1), the great question in v. 8 should be interpreted as follows: "When the Son of man comes (whether in judgment on a nation or at the End) will he find this faith in Him that revealed itself in a waiting upon the Lord in persevering prayer?" [11]

(b) *Biblical unity also requires that the details of a passage should be viewed in the light of the main thought of that passage, while that passage should in turn be viewed in the light of the main message of the book in which it is found.*

Example: Rev. 1:12-18. The main thought here is: the glory of the resurrected Christ in the midst of His struggling Church on earth. Mark how every detail helps to accentuate this truth: the long robe, the golden girdle round the breast . . . the eyes like a flame of fire, etc. This passage in turn expresses in its own peculiar way something of the great message of the book of Revelation as a whole, expressed by H. B. Swete as follows: "The whole book is a *Sursum corda*, inviting the churches to seek strength in the faith of a triumphant and returning Christ".[12]

(c) *The preacher should compare Scripture with Scripture, provided he compares portions that deal with the same subject.* Difficult parts of Scripture should be explained with the help of clear parts, and not *vice versa.*

The preacher should first of all look for clear parts in the *same book* in which the difficult portion is found. Thus, e.g., the difficult portion about the rider on the white horse in Rev. 6 can be better understood with the help of another portion in the same book, namely chap. 19, where the name of the rider is clearly mentioned (cf. vv. 11, 13, 16). Where there is no such clear passage in the same book, it will be wise to look for a clear passage in another book by the *same* author. (Thus the difficult expression of Paul in I Tim. 1:20 about delivering somebody to Satan becomes clearer when we compare I Cor. 5:5, where it is at least certain that Paul was thinking of very severe disciplinary steps which aimed at the person's eventual conversion.) Only thereafter should we look for any clear part in any other book that may throw some light on a difficult passage.

3. *Thirdly the Bible comes to us with divine clarity.*

The one authoritative Word of God is a clear Word. By the clarity of the Bible we do not mean a formal clearness by which we are able to grasp the meaning of Scripture apart from a living faith in Jesus Christ. "The clarity of Scripture is the clarity of God Himself as seen by the believer on the face of Jesus Christ through the illumination of the Holy Spirit."[13] This means that a clever man, following all the rules laid down for the understanding of the Scriptures, without the guidance of the Holy Spirit will understand nothing of what it is all about (cf. I Cor. 2:10-14). It also means that a little child, knowing very little of rules of exegesis, will be able, through the enlightenment of the Holy Spirit, to grasp the essence of the biblical message (cf. Psa. 119:130).

To mention only two implications for preaching:

(*a*) While making use of all kinds of tools to enable him to explain his text fully, the preacher will above all, and through all of this, seek the guidance of the Holy Spirit through much prayer.[14]

(*b*) The Holy Spirit has been given to the Church as a whole. In its confessions of faith the Church explains the biblical message as she understands it, under the guidance of the Holy Spirit. Thus, although such confessions of faith are never infallible as the Bible itself, the minister of the Gospel will make use of them in guiding him towards a correct understanding of the main contents of Scripture.[15]

4. *Fourthly, the Bible is both divinely necessary and divinely sufficient unto salvation.*

We confess these two perfections of Scripture in the closest connection with Jesus Christ as its central message. Firstly: since there is no salvation outside Christ (John 14:6), it follows that the Bible which brings us this message with divine authority, is a divine necessity. Secondly: since salvation in Jesus Christ means life eternal, it follows that the Bible, which was written to tell us this, is divinely sufficient unto salvation (cf. John 20:30-31, II Tim. 3:16-17, I John 1:1-4).

From the necessity and sufficiency of Scripture follow the conclusion that we should preach, as our Reformed fathers said, *sola Scriptura et tota Scriptura*. *Only* the Scriptures—thus not what the preacher deems fit to preach. *All* the Scriptures—thus not only certain beloved portions! (cf. Acts 20:27).

IV. The Bible shows us that God's revelation in Jesus Christ came as salvation history.

God's revelation is not to be understood as a timeless and supra-historical event: it is a revelation in history.[16] This truth is beautifully expressed in answer 19 of the Heidelberg Catechism, which speaks of "the holy Gospel, which God Himself revealed in the beginning in the Garden of Eden, afterward proclaimed through the holy patriarchs and prophets and foreshadowed through the sacrifices and other rites of the Old Covenant, and finally fulfilled through His own well-beloved Son" (cf. Heb. 1:1, 11:40). The history told in the Bible is the history of God's great deeds of salvation in and through Jesus Christ. This is *salvation history*—the history of the incarnation (or "enfleshment") of the Word. This implies that all preaching is essentially salvation-historical preaching: *it deals with some moment or moments in the history of salvation,* which in turn implies that *the preacher should take God's salvation history seriously.*

How this could be done may be explained in the following five ways:

1. The preacher may not spiritualise Scripture at random.

Gen. 22:5. "Then Abraham said to his young men, Stay here with the ass; I and the lad will go yonder and worship . . ." A minister once explained these words as follows: Abraham and his son are representatives of diligent Christians who are willing to ascend the mountain of faith, while the young men at the foot of the mountain are symbolic of lukewarm Christians, who prefer to stay with an ass rather than to accept the challenge to climb the mountain of faith.

Well, if the staying with the ass implies lukewarmness, then Abraham, the diligent man of God, should get a reprimand for having given a command to others to stay lukewarm! And when in the last part of the text Abraham said that he and the son *would return* to the young men, the diligent man of God should get a reprimand for planning *in advance* to become lukewarm again! It is typical of this type of exposition that people in the course of salvation history who were actually doing something good (like the young men in this case), are made the symbol of something bad, just to fit the preacher's own thought-scheme.[17]

2. The preacher will search for the salvation-historical meaning of the text as provided by its immediate and wider historical context.

A text falls within a certain period of time within God's history of salvation, and every such period has its own specific theological meaning or "theological horizon", as E. Clowney has pointed out.[18]

Example: I Sam. 17 (David and Goliath). Indeed, as Clowney says, one hears sermons on this theme that might almost as well have been preached on Jack the Giant Killer. There is a slight improvement when David's faith is stressed. So often, each of the five stones that David picked up has to represent one of many possible characteristics of the young lad. But when we enquire about the salvation-historical meaning of the text, as provided by the historical setting, the narrative is viewed in a new light.

I Sam. 17 forms part of the history of the kings of Israel. The special theological meaning of this period within God's history of salvation is this: God wanted to establish the theocracy (*i.e.* His reign on earth) by choosing and anointing David as king of His people. This means that the more immediate historical context of chap. 17 (David's anointing in I Sam. 16) and the wider historical context (the great promise given to David before his death, namely that there would always be an offspring to sit on his throne, II Sam. 7:12-16) enable us to see I Sam. 17 in its true light. The true theocratic king would be that one who would come in the Name of the God of Israel, who would obey Him, who would long to make known His glory among the nations. David's mighty words to

Goliath in I Sam. 17:45-47 show us that he himself was well aware of this. His anointing by Samuel in I Sam. 16 brought this home to him! (v. 13). His victory over Goliath would testify to all the earth that there is but one God—the Lord of the hosts of Israel. In this context, the five little stones are expressive of his faith that not by the sword, but by the power of the Lord the victory will be gained. As soon as these stones insist on becoming more than that, we should rather throw them back to where David picked them up long ago.

3. *The relation of the text with Jesus Christ, the centre of God's revelation, should be shown in a way that fully honours the historical situation of which the text speaks.*

Let us take the Song of Solomon as an example. Certainly this book, within the context of the whole of Scripture Canon, proclaims the love between Yahweh and His people, and the love between Christ and His bride, the Church. But this may not be proclaimed to the exclusion of the fact that this is, first of all, a song about a *real marriage* between Solomon and the one bride whom he really loved. In other words, *it is exactly in their married life that man and woman must show forth the love between Christ and His bride, the Church* (cf. Eph. 5:22-23). If this is borne in mind, how immensely concrete can the message of this book become for the congregation![19]

It would be a mistake to think that Christ is to be found in every detail of an O.T. book; but it is equally a mistake to think that He is to be found only in a few Messianic texts. This would disregard the fact that Christ is the centre of the whole of God's revelation as given in the Bible.[20] Take, e.g., the Book *Ecclesiastes*. In spite of its difficulties, it clearly shows the complete futility of everything under the sun if God is not in it. In this peculiar way it cries for God in Christ, in whom alone man has an imperishable pearl of great price, and in whom alone man's life becomes eternally significant.[21]

By honouring the historical distance between the original situation and today, a better exposition is given and in reality a sharper application, as a brief word on Psa. 84 may show. The preacher may here be tempted to fall away with something like the following: "Like the poet of Psa. 84, we should also long to enter the courts of the Lord, *i.e.* to go to church on the day of the Lord." This is not wholly wrong, but such preaching easily leads to an unbiblical moralistic type of preaching—an exhortation to the congregation, cut loose from the roots of grace clearly implied in the text. Salvation-historical preaching however, will proceed more or less upon these lines: 'The psalmist was living in the times of the old dispensation, when the pious Israelite had the right to enter only the forecourt of the temple, and that normally only once a year. This made him jealous of the sparrows and swallows who made their nests inside the temple at the altar of the God of hosts (v. 3). But the O.T. believer's desire has been fulfilled in Jesus Christ. Since His coming the inner sanctuary of communion with God stands open always and everywhere, for every believer to enter. What wealth we possess! With such wealth of grace surrounding us, how dare we neglect to meet together regularly?"[22]

4. *The preacher will accept TYPOLOGY as an integral part of the true understanding of salvation history.*

This is something quite different from haphazard spiritualising. The following definition may help us to see the right as well as the limits of typology: it is a person or event especially in the O.T., pointing to something more, especially in the N.T., *but then in such a way that the so-called type in the O.T. is itself an indispensable preparatory link in the historical line that leads to that something more which is to come.* Whereas wilful spiritualising ignores and even destroys the meaning of an event within its historical context, typology honours the historical moment and indicates how it points to something more that is to come.[23]

Example: When David killed Goliath, he acted as type of the greater David, who was to come forth from David's seed, to conquer every enemy and establish the Kingdom in his own person. But mark how this event in I Sam. 17, where David acts as a type of Christ, is an indispensable historical link in the chain of salvation history: if Goliath had conquered David, then God's promise that the Messiah would come from David's seed would have been destroyed, and no salvation would have been obtained for anybody.

5. *The preacher will show awareness of the close connection between salvation history and world history.*

With salvation history God broke into world history, thereby creating a unique history somehow intertwined with world history in such a way that three relationships become visible:

(*a*) Salvation history somehow includes world history;

(*b*) it gives world history a full chance to develop towards its godless goal: the appearance of antichrist;

(*c*) it completely controls and completes world history. God made Jesus Christ head of His Church, but He also made our Mediator head of the universe for the sake of His Church on earth. "History is *His* story."

It is especially the last book of the Bible that brings to the fore this three-fold relationship between salvation history and world history. The Lamb has been found worthy to open and fulfil the book of God's counsel with regard to the Church as well as the world (Rev. 5). Thus the preacher ought to be acquainted with salvation history and Church history, but also with "secular" history. In this way he will be able to help the congregation to see how God who was and who is at work in salvation history, is at work in secular history as well.

This the preacher will do without making the grave mistake of thinking that prophecies of Scripture provide us with a chronological history written in advance. Of all the books of the Bible, the last one has had to suffer most in this connection. Basic to the understanding of this difficult book is, that instead of giving us a chronological history in advance, it traverses history time and again from the first to the second coming of our Lord, though with ever increasing intensity.[24]

V. God's salvation history with Christ as its centre takes the form of a covenant history.

When we speak of salvation history, we speak of covenant history, for the whole of the Gospel of God in Jesus Christ takes the form of a covenant of grace, from Genesis to Revelation. This means that all that has been said up to now must be viewed within the framework of this covenant of grace. (It is very interesting to note how much attention has recently been paid to the covenant idea in biblical studies as a result of the discoveries of Ancient Near Eastern Treaties.[25] For ages it was only Reformation Theology of the Calvinistic type that accepted the covenant idea as an inherent part of theology.)

For preaching, this implies that the preacher is always in some way busy with covenant preaching. Christians are being urged to live up to the standards of the covenant of grace, unbelievers are being urged to enter this covenant, outside of which there is no salvation. If all our preaching is really covenant preaching, it will have a sound influence on the way we preach about the *LAW* of God. How many good Christians are there who find it difficult to accept that the O.T. is already essentially Gospel and not simply one continuous preaching of the law? And is this not in part because many preachers preach the law as law, *severed from its essential covenant-of-grace frame within which alone it ought to be understood?*[26] Church members may benefit greatly from the careful reading of the following Scripture portions in the given order: Exod. 20:2, Exod. 2:23-25, Gen. 12:3, Gal. 3:26, 3:17.

VI. Covenant history is a progressive history, basically proceeding from covenant promise in the books of the old covenant to covenant fulfilment in the books of the new covenant.

Many books and articles have been written on the very important question of the relation between the Old and the New Testament. We believe that it is correct to say with many that the O.T. is basically covenant promise and the N.T. basically covenant fulfilment. The O.T. is *basically* promise, for it is not promise only, but also contains some fulfilment;

84

and the N.T. is *basically* fulfilment, for the N.T. in turn points to the final consummation of all things. And yet there is a progressiveness in salvation history which finds in Jesus Christ so great and final a fulfilment, that the O.T. can be called promise and the New the fulfilment. As F. F. Bruce puts it: "Jesus has fulfilled the ancient promises, and in fulfilling them He has given them a new meaning, in which their original meaning is not set aside but caught up into something more comprehensive and far reaching than was foreseen before He came".[27]

Because covenant history from the beginning of the Old Testament to the end of the New Testament is a progressive history, it follows that this history is right from the start directed towards the END, *i.e.* covenant history is *eschatological* history. Time and again something of the End is revealed along the way.

This means that *all preaching is essentially eschatological. With regard to the O.T.,* people should see that a great part of the permanent value of the O.T. consists in this: that all along the way it thrusts through prophetically to the End, including both first and second coming. In other words, although *historically* it leads us to a point a few hundred years before Christ, *prophetically* it leads us to the very end (although of course in an O.T. garb). Think of direct prophetical passages like Isa. 24 and 66 and Dan. 7, but also of historical parts with a typical meaning, pointing to the end. Thus when in Exod. 14 and 15 Israel under Moses sings its song of victory after the miraculous exodus from Egypt, then all this is typical of God's people of the End-time under their great Moses, Christ, singing their song of glory to God because of the complete victory over the Pharaoh of the End-time, the Antichrist (cf. Rev. 15:2-3).

With regard to preaching from *the New Testament,* two things should be stressed:

1. *People should understand that in Jesus Christ the great End has already come.* He is *HO ESCHATOS,* the great LAST ONE,[28] the fulfilment of the Covenant, the last Adam. His time is the time between the first and the second coming, *i.e.* the last days. With His resurrection He has introduced the new *aion,* the new "age". In Him the new heaven and the new earth are here already, although they are yet to come.

And now, what happened to Christ has happened to us, His body at Calvary, in the resurrection and in the ascension. Yes, "God . . . made us alive together with Christ . . . and raised us up with him, and made us sit with him in the heavenly places in Christ Jesus . . ." (Eph. 2:5). Therefore, if anybody is in Christ, he is not only a new creature (as the word in II Cor. 5:17 may be translated) but also new *creation.* Together with God's people, he is already an integral part of God's new heaven

85

and earth, however much the opposite may *seem* to be the case amid earthly trials.

2. *The preacher will take care of the fact that from the birth to the death of our Lord there is a kind of overlapping of the Old and New Covenant.*

In Christ the New Covenant has come, but from His birth to His death He brought everything for which the O.T. stood to its very climax. Born under the Law (Gal. 4:4), He lived to fulfil the law (Matt. 5:17). In other words, in the gospels the preacher has to take double care about the place of a text in the history of salvation.

Example: Luke 23:56. When it is here said that the women rested on the sabbath day according to the commandment, then from this it may not be inferred that we still ought to rest on the Jewish Sabbath, for the change would only come with the *resurrection*. Until the time of Jesus' resurrection everything was still wrapped in its O.T. form. But thereafter the great change would become apparent.

VII. The grand purpose of salvation history as covenant history is the coming of the Kingdom of God.

The Covenant can be called the *road* along which salvation history runs, the Kingdom can be called its *destination*. Right from the very start, God's covenant history with Israel was a history for the sake of God's royal rule in and through Jesus Christ, established and acknowledged in the lives of His elect from Israel and from *all* other nations by the regenerating power of the Holy Spirit (Gen. 12:3, Isa. 2:2-4, 49:6). "Covenant administration is Kingdom administration."[29] "If we do not want to do mission work," a minister once said to his congregation, "then we had better tear Matt. 28:19 out of our Bibles." His intention was good, but he ought rather to have said to his people: "You had better tear up the *whole* Bible if you refuse to support mission work, for the whole Bible is a mission book from Genesis to Revelation". It is the book of God's coming to us through the coming of His Son. His Son was *sent* into the world to tell all the world of this sending, this mission of the Son to the world for the sake of the world. God's book is therefore a Kingdom book. Says J. Bright: "The concept of the Kingdom of God involves in a real sense the total message of the Bible".[30]

The implication with regard to preaching is clear: every sermon is basically a mission sermon, in the sense that it deals with the mission of the Son to this world for the sake of this world. The prayer underlying every sermon is: "Let Thy Kingdom come, for Thine *is* the Kingdom, the power and the glory . . .". Because the Reformed minister believes with all his heart that the Kingdom belongs to God, he will pray and preach and work with all his heart that this Kingdom may come *intensively* in the heart of every convert and *extensively* among all nations. Through his preaching the Reformed minister will, in the Name of his Lord, put before God's people nothing more and nothing less than this as their task: to pray and give and live and work . . . for the Kingdom.

VIII. Scripture's Kingdom message to man gives glory to God.

The purpose of salvation history along the covenant road is the establishment of the Kingdom of God. And the aim of the Kingdom is *"Gloria in excelsis Deo*—glory to God in the highest". To live the life of the Kingdom is to live a life of praise.[31]

With regard to preaching, this means that by the grace of God the preacher and his sermon should be caught up in a witness which is nothing less than a doxology, a hymn of praise to God, an act of worship. "What strikes you about the preachers of the New Testament is that they had been swept off their feet and carried away by the glory of the great revelation" (J. S. Stewart).

May God grant that in a time such as this His Church may have ministers whose lives and preaching reflect the glory of the *Word* of God—and thus of the *God* of the Word. For:

> *"To Him who sits upon the Throne*
> *and to the Lamb*
> *be blessing and honour*
> *and glory and might*
> *for ever and ever!"*

---

1 *Revolt,* p. 183.
2 Cf. William C. Fletcher, *The Moderns,* 1962, p. 114.
3 Hamilton, *Revolt,* p. 181.
4 Cf. *Ibid.,* pp. 124, 183.
5 Cf. D .O. Fuller, *Spurgeon's Lectures to his Students,* 1945, p. 284.
6 See Edmund P. Clowney, *Preaching and Biblical Theology,* London, 1962, p. 74; T. Hoekstra, *Gereformeerde Homiletiek,* Wageningen, p. 172.
7 K. Dijk, *Over de Laatste Dingen,* Vol. III, 1962, pp. 200, 203; S. Greidanus, *Sola Scriptura* (Problems and Principles in preaching historical Texts), 1970, pp. 224-226.
8 See H. U. von Balthasar, *Herrlichkeit,* Vol. I, 1961, p. 421; G. C. Berkouwer, *De Wederkomst van Christus,* Vol. II, 1963, pp. 186; K. Dijk, *De Dienst der Prediking,* 1955, pp. 82-84.
9 Cf. L. Berkhof, *Manual of Christian Doctrine,* 1933, pp. 42-43.
10 Cf. T. Hoekstra, *Homiletiek,* pp. 201-203; K. Dijk, *Dienst,* pp. 90-93.
11 See e.g. I. H. Marshall, in *The New Bible Commentary,* 1970, *ad loc.*
12 *The Apocalypse of St. John,* 1908, p. xcvi.
13 H. W. Rossouw in his doctoral thesis *Klaarheid en Interpretasie,* 1963, p. 250.
14 Spurgeon, *Lectures,* p. 275.
15 Cf. W. D. Jonker, *Eksegese en Dogmatiek* in: Hermeneutica, Pretoria, 1970, ch. 9.

16 G. C. Berkouwer, *De Heilige Schrift,* Vol. I, 1966, p. 29.

17 For examples from the Church Fathers, see F. W. Farrar, *History of Interpretation* (Bampton Lectures, 1885), Gr. Rapids, 1961.

18 *Preaching,* p. 75.

19 This has been well shown in a Dutch commentary by L. H. van der Meiden (*Het Hooglied,* Baarn, no date).

20 See the beautiful paragraph in H. Veldkamp, *Amos-Obadja* (Paraphrase der Heilige Schrift), p. 12-13.

21 Cf. G. Ch. Aalders, *De Prediker* (Korte Verklaring der Heilige Schrift), 1958, p. 18.

22 An example taken from Prof. B. Holwenda's chapter on salvation history in preaching in *"Begonnen hebbende van Mozes . . .",* 1953, p. 111. For a good discussion, with examples, see the important work of J. Bright, *The Authority of the Old Testament,* 1967, chaps. 4 and 5. Cf. also Greidanus, *Sola Scriptura.*

23 Cf. L. Berkhof, *Principles of Biblical Interpretation,* 1960, pp. 144-148; P. A. Verhoef, *Some Notes on Typological Exegesis* in: New Light on some O.T. Problems, Pretoria, 1962, pp. 58-63; B. Ramm, *Protestant Biblical Interpretation,* 1956, ch. 9; A. B. Mickelsen, *Interpreting the Bible,* 1963, ch. 11; Francis Foulkes, "Typology or Allegory?" in *Themelios,* II. 2, pp. 8-15; W. Eichrodt, *Is Typological Exegesis an appropriate Method?* in: Essays on O.T. Interpretation (ed. C. Westermann), 1963, ch. 11.

24 Cf. Wm. Hendriksen, *More than Conquerors,* 1962, ch. 2, who with R. C. H. Lenski *et al* accepts *seven* parallels. In the writer's opinion there are more than seven.

25 The bibliography is overwhelming. For orientation, see K. A. Kitchen, *Ancient Orient and Old Testament,* 1966, pp. 90-102; Prof. F. C. Fensham of S.A. recently wrote *Treaty and Law in the Bible and the Ancient Near East* (with much recent bibliography), to be published by Blackwell in the course of 1971 (perhaps under a slightly different name).

26 For an able illustration, see J. Bright, *Authority,* pp. 214-218. For beautiful paragraphs on covenant and law, see J. A. Heyns, *Die Nuwe mens onderweg,* Cape Town, 1970, pp. 24-33.

27 Biblical Exegesis and the Qumran Texts (series: Exegetica), 1959, p. 77. Cf. also Bruce, *This is That* (The N.T. Development of some O.T. Themes), 1968, p. 21. A beautiful chapter on "Promise and Fulfilment" is found in G. C. Berkouwer, *The Person of Christ,* 1954, pp. 113-152. With regard to the implications for the exegesis of O.T. Prophecy, see the lucid remarks in Erroll Hulse's *The Restoration of Israel,* 1968, pp. 25-29.

28 For a new, thorough-going study in this respect, see the Afrikaans doctoral thesis of A. König, *Jesus Christus die Eschatos,* 1970, 569 pp.

29 M. Kline, *Law Covenant,* Westm. Theol. Journal, XXVII/1 (1964), p. 17.

30 *The Kingdom of God,* 1953, p. 7.

31 On life as praise, see Claus Westermann, *The Praise of God in the Psalms,* 1960, pp. 158-162; N. H. Ridderbos, *De Plaats van het Loven en van het Bidden in het O.T.,* Kampen, 1970.